BUILDING CITY SCENERY

for your model railroad

John Pryke

KALMBACH
BOOKS

Acknowledgments

Building model cities is a big job. Over the last $2\frac{1}{2}$ years, this book has taken my full-time effort and the part-time contributions of some fine modelers to complete it. For their efforts, I extend the following acknowledgments: Bill Vaughan, who has helped me since the book was started, for his tireless efforts during construction and photography and his ingenious development of our photo backdrops. Chuck Miller, for decorating and constructing all those two-story buildings and storefronts. Guy Hutchings, for painting enough crates, barrels, trash, and junk to fill a city. Vic Hamburger, who somehow painted more than 150 people and 20 vehicles in four weeks, during his "spare time." Marty Klein, for taking on and finishing all those left-over modeling tasks. Beverly and Bob Shea, for letting me photograph their exquisite city module. Bob Leavitt, for allowing me to drape extension cords over his excellent pike so I could photograph his urban craftsmanship. And last, but by no means least, my wife Sandy, for putting up with all my hours in the basement, behind the camera, and on the computer, which has made her feel like a model railroad widow.

Printed in Canada

04 05 06 07 08   10 9 8 7 6 5 4 3

Visit our website at
http://kalmbachbooks.com
Secure online ordering available

Publisher's Cataloging-in-Publication
(Provided by Quality Books, Inc.)

Pryke, John.
    Building city scenery for model railroads /
John Pryke. — 1st ed.
    p. cm.
    ISBN: 0-89024-343-3

    I. Railroads—Models. I. Title.

TF197.P79 2000   625.1'9
                        QBI99-1900

Book design: Mark Watson
Cover design: Kristi Ludwig

Contents

Preface

When I built my first city on my HO layout in a New York apartment in 1949, its buildings were printed cardstock with cellophane windows. The traffic consisted of a mixture of metal cars, trucks, and buses of moderate detail (in several different scales), and the people were featureless metal and plastic globs. The streets were painted plywood, and there were a few over-sized streetlights. But that was state of the art, and I was proud of it.

By 1976 I was building a city with buildings kitbashed from two Heljan Breweries (the most American-looking, large plastic structure on the market) and a few small plastic and cardstock urban-looking kits. The vehicles and figures on the market were injection-molded plastic or cast metal, and there were even some good street details available. I thought things had come a long way in 30 years; but I had no idea of what the future held!

Today, hundreds of urban building kits in a wide variety of architectural styles are available in all scales. Highly detailed, easy-to-assemble styrene, urethane, or Hydrocal kits at reasonable prices outshine anything available in the past. Where a kit will not fit the available space, you can build custom structures using plastic modular building components. Beautifully detailed cars, trucks, and buses are available whether you model the 1930s or the present day. There are thousands of jewel-like miniature figures in a host of realistic poses to populate your city; and the smallest details are available for your buildings and streets. Urban modeling has come of age—the real challenge is putting all of the pieces together.

This book focuses on how to build that city of your dreams. I'll start by describing some of the forms that it can take to suit the railroad you've built (or are building). I'll discuss techniques to make your city look big, even if you only have a little space. Next, I'll show you how to decorate, detail, and weather your buildings so they look like the real thing; and how to include all the things you need to make your city live—people on the sidewalks, street details, and trash in the alleys. And then I'll discuss some new techniques, like using photographs of real city buildings and a personal computer to make your city backdrops.

By the time you have finished your first city, I hope that you will have as much fun building it as I have had writing this book. Let's get started!

John Pryke
June 1999

HOW A CITY GROWS

Railroads have always been an integral part of the urban scene. In early days cities grew along the railroad lines. Today, railroads run along the periphery of the modern civic center, through industrial and commercial districts where low-rise older structures proliferate. Here, on New York's West Side Freight Line, an RS-3 pauses within sight of the Empire State Building and midtown high-rise offices.

Before we start to build a city for your model railroad, we need to look at the relationship between real cities and real railroads. Since its invention in 1829, the railroad has been a key part of the urban scene. Cities grow along transportation lines from the center outward. In the early 1800s, New York, Albany, Philadelphia, and New Orleans initially grew because of seaport, canal, or river locations. With the advent of the railroad in the 1830s, Chicago, Atlanta, and many other inland cities developed as a result of this new form of transportation. For the next 150 years cities grew along and around the railroad lines that linked them and provided fast freight and passenger transportation.

While proximity to rail lines is one way to measure a city's development, its architecture is another. The oldest buildings in today's city are brick structures in which the external walls bear all of the weight. This form of construction rarely supports buildings higher than eight stories. During the 1800s, numerous brick structures—mills, factories, warehouses, and tenements—were built alongside the railroads. Many survive today.

By 1910 a new generation of buildings had appeared, with an internal support skeleton made of steel (and later reinforced concrete). Structural steel allowed buildings to grow vertically, so skyscraper office buildings and apartments higher

Fig. I-1. The Milwaukee Road's streamlined *Hiawatha* snakes down the main line near the center of Milwaukee in the late 1930s. Old brick industrial buildings and tenements line the route, a testament to the noise and soot generated by the railroad.

Fig. I-2. A New York Central "express" chugs down the middle of Washington Street in Syracuse, New York, in the mid 1930s. Pedestrians, automobiles, and streetcars all had to compete with the railroad.

Fig. I-3. Grand Central Terminal in 1906. Even though electrified third rail is being installed, trains are still steam-powered, and smoke blots out all but the tallest buildings. This was a common sight in the middle of U.S. cities in the first part of the century. Even though the railroad was the primary transportation in the United States, it was an eyesore in the middle of the city.

Fig. I-4. View of the 2-mile-long approach tunnel under Park Avenue to the new Grand Central Terminal in New York City. In this 1953 view, the five-story tenements still stand along the railroad cut.

than 15 stories sprang up in the city center where land was at a premium. The walls of these buildings hung like curtains from the steel skeleton and not only kept out the elements, but also were a showcase for the architecture of the time.

During the 1920s and '30s tall masonry or stone-faced buildings dominated the city scene; and art deco, a modern variant of classical European architecture, appeared. New York's Chrysler Building with its spike and stainless steel gargoyles has been called the ultimate art-deco structure. In the 1950s glass and stainless steel exteriors appeared; today, city centers reflect these newer forms of architecture.

Outside the downtown area, cavernous factories and warehouses constructed of concrete with brick panels and steel sash windows extend outward into the suburbs. Many of these buildings were built next to railroads for access to the primary form of transportation and slowly replaced the older mill buildings.

Where the City Meets the Railroad

Although the railroad has been a key component of commerce for over a century, it's a noisy, sooty, and not very desirable next-door neighbor. Consequently, railroads in urban areas were surrounded by factories or run-down tenements (see fig. I-1),

many of which exist today. In some cases the city and the railroad became one, with main lines running down city streets (see fig. I-2). In the city center, the railroads built grand terminals with marble interiors, but the associated yards were a sooty blot all too near plush downtown offices (see fig. I-3).

Cities across the country reacted differently to minimize the aesthetic drawbacks of the railroad. After several serious accidents in the smoke-filled tunnel approach to Grand Central Terminal, New York passed a law prohibiting the operation of steam locomotives south of the Harlem River after 1908. The New York Central Railroad, then design-

Photo by Burdell Bulgrin

Fig. I-5. Milwaukee train no. 117 departs Chicago. Here, the main line through the city runs in a cut behind older brick buildings and, in the distance, under newer glass and high-rise offices. While not as completely invisible as in a tunnel, the railroad is still hidden to the greatest extent possible in the city center, and only older buildings abut it where it is visible.

Photo by Herbert H. Harwood Jr.

Fig. I-6. A Jersey Central Whitcomb switcher hitches a ride on a car float down New York City's Harlem River in 1955. Like many other railroads in the New York area, the Jersey Central depended on a fleet of carfloats and tugs to move freight cars from its main railhead to small, isolated transfer yards all around the busy harbor.

ing a new terminal, decided to electrify it with 600-volt third rail. The huge, two-level station was hidden underground and air rights over the tracks were sold to building developers. With the railroad underground the old tenements vanished and high-rise offices and apartments took their place (see fig. I-4). Other cities chose to elevate the main lines, but the noise was still there and the "railroad slums" persisted.

However, burying or elevating railroads was not practical in all cities. Chicago, which depended on rail traffic for its lifeblood, ran most of its railroads through cuts or behind buildings (see fig. I-5). Along the prestigious lakefront, the Illinois Central's yards survived until the 1970s, when the city finally reclaimed this valuable land for new skyscrapers. In San Francisco, the Southern Pacific's Townsend Street Terminal was on the surface, but the high-rise city center began several blocks away, so the railroad remained surrounded by older structures.

Even though railroads were hidden in the city center, they continued to be visible and thrive in urban industrial areas and on the waterfront. Small transfer lines surrounded New York harbor (see fig. I-6); in-street freight operations ran in Portland, Maine, and Salt Lake City; and Milwaukee's "Beer Line" still moves cars between giant breweries. Regardless of the period or location, building a city is a fascinating subject for the model railroader.

Building the Big City for Your Model Railroad

No matter how large or small your layout, you can create a big city effect. But before you start choosing buildings or naming streets, there are several planning steps you'll want to take:

• Decide how much layout space to devote to a city. This can range from a foot or two of backdrop to a complete urban railroad.

• Decide how much city you want on your railroad and how much railroad you want in your city. In the first case it may only be a freight yard with a city in the background. In the second it can range from a station or a terminal to an urban freight line with in-street operation.

• Pick a prototype city if you want one. If you live near or remember a particular city, you may want to give your model city the look and feel of the prototype.

• Draw up a good set of plans showing how the city fits into your layout. This should include track plans; streets that go over or under your main line; and buildings, which can range from freestanding structures, to flats, to a printed backdrop.

• Build your city. Use commercially available kits as is, or kitbash several together to achieve the look and feel of a favorite building or cityscape.

• Modify or rebuild your city to suit your needs. As new urban kits come out you may want to replace old ones. You may wish to change the period you model by incorporating newer (or older) architecture.

In the following chapters, you'll see the different elements you can use to build your city scenery. You'll discover that there are many different ways to add a city to your model railroad. Finally, you'll see how to detail buildings, streets, vehicles, people, trash, and junk—everything that makes your city come alive and achieve maximum realism.

This city scene contains all the elements you can use to build a city on your model railroad: full buildings, partial buildings, flats, and a backdrop. Note how these different elements, plus their different types of architecture, combine to give added realism.

**DESIGNING A CITY
CHAPTER 1**

The Primary Elements of Model Railroad City Scenery

Photo by Dave Frary

The primary elements of a city are its buildings, whether they are high-rise offices, industrial structures, commercial buildings, or residences. How you choose to construct and arrange these buildings can dramatically alter the look of a city on your model railroad. In this chapter, we'll look at a variety of kits and modular building components and then discuss the different ways to model buildings—as complete structures, partial structures, flats, and backdrops. Using these techniques, you'll see how to create a realistic model railroad city landscape or, if you will, a *cityscape* on your pike.

What Is Available

When I built my first large cityscape in 1976, there were only a few urban structures on the market. Heljan made a very large brewery kit in plastic that many of my friends had used for city structures. So I bought two, cut them up, made half a dozen different buildings out of them, and painted each a different color of brick. While the buildings all had similar architecture, they looked pretty good as a whole. Today, many manufacturers produce hundreds of city buildings in all scales as kits or in modular component form. The different types of industrial, commercial, and residential architecture (brick, steel-framed, and reinforced concrete, described in the Introduction) that abut urban railroads are well represented in highly detailed plastic, urethane, or Hydrocal. In general, you have only to assemble these buildings, paint them, and place them on your railroad to create the look and feel of a real city. If there is no kit that exactly matches your requirements, you can easily revamp or kitbash kit parts or use modular building components to create a unique structure. In addition, there are a number of *flats* (drawings glued on cardboard or castings of building walls) and *backdrops* that depict urban structures and add depth to your cityscape. An appendix at the back of the book provides a list of manufacturers that make urban structures, vehicles, and details in different model railroad scales.

Most of the urban structures currently on the market cover the time from the late 1800s to the 1960s. With the exception of a very few offerings in HO and N scales, the only types of structures not readily available are modern, high-rise office buildings. There are two reasons for this absence. First, most model railroads (in HO or larger scales) do not have the space for the foundation or the vertical height needed by large,

Photo by Dave Frary

Fig. 1-1. We are looking across the roofs of low-rise buildings into Atlantic Avenue and the taller commercial buildings across the street. Having to look over a series of structures to see the main scene is an excellent way to make the viewer feel that he or she is right in the model city.

high-rise structures. Second, the majority of these buildings are in the city center, either well away from the railroad, or where the right of way is hidden in a tunnel or a deep cut.

If you model in some scale besides HO or N, and want to have high-rise buildings, you will probably have to scratchbuild them. An excellent article titled "Modeling High Rise Buildings" by Mike Palmiter appeared in the August 1992 issue of *Model Railroader* magazine. The excerpted article printed to the right shows how to use a Plexiglas shell, mat board, and vinyl strips to construct modern, high-rise buildings in any scale.

Representing Buildings Different Ways in Your Cityscape

When you build a cityscape, the construction and arrangement of the buildings will determine its realism and impact on the viewer. Most model cityscapes are a combination of several different representations of buildings: *Complete buildings* have walls on all sides and a roof. *Partial*

buildings have walls only on those sides that can be seen, plus a roof. *Flats,* which are single walls, are usually standing in front of a backdrop; they are printed paper mounted on cardboard or three-dimensional wall castings. *Backdrops* are pictures of groups of buildings on a wall or other vertical background surface.

Where to Use Complete Buildings

Complete buildings work best when all sides of the building can be seen. This occurs in the very forefront of a cityscape, usually next to the railroad's trackwork, see fig. 1-4, or at the edge of a layout. Wherever possible, I construct complete buildings from kits or modular building components. If it's large enough, a building can fill an entire block. Most urban structures, however, are smaller; their backs face an alley with another building just behind it. One effective way to use a complete building is as a low-rise structure on a street. Placing the structure next to the sidewalk and using higher buildings behind it makes the scene look

Photo by Mike Palmiter, courtesy of *Model Railroader* magazine

These impressive skyscrapers were built using Mike Palmiter's technique.

MAKING MODERN CITY STRUCTURES
Plexiglas Skyscrapers

The first step in making a high-rise building is to mark the desired overall wall dimensions on a piece of Plexiglas. Score the outline with a utility knife, then snap the piece apart over the edge of a counter. After cutting the walls, apply glue and join the four main sides as shown (upper right). Be sure to add bracing to ensure that your building won't come apart later when being handled.

Next, you'll want to add windows, as well as architectural trim, to the basic shell using strips of mat board and vinyl tape (lower right). Keep in mind that the scale of your building is determined by the width and spacing of the horizontal floor separators. Prototype building floors are generally 10 to 15 feet apart, depending on the style of architecture. For HO scale models, using ½"-wide tape spaced roughly ½" to ¾" apart scales to about 9 feet. For S or O scale models, you'll want to use even wider dimensions.

The last step of this construction method is to affix the verticals, which can be strips of any width of wood, cardstock, or mat board. The verticals can be wide, narrow, or both, depending on the style of building you're modeling.

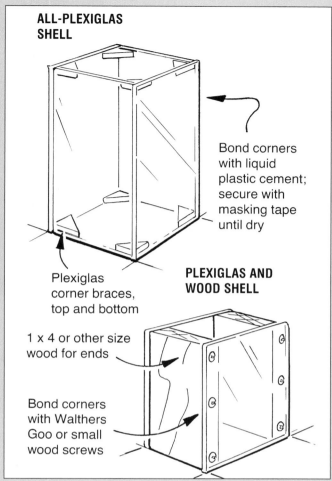

ALL-PLEXIGLAS SHELL

Bond corners with liquid plastic cement; secure with masking tape until dry

Plexiglas corner braces, top and bottom

PLEXIGLAS AND WOOD SHELL

1 x 4 or other size wood for ends

Bond corners with Walthers Goo or small wood screws

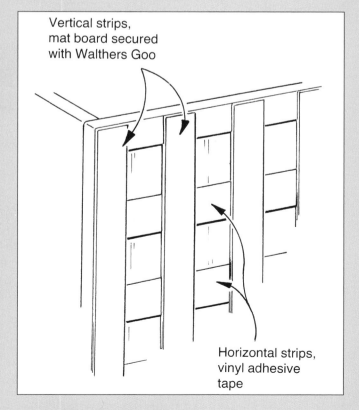

Vertical strips, mat board secured with Walthers Goo

Horizontal strips, vinyl adhesive tape

Fig. 1-2. Several different kinds of urban back lots appear in this photo. From left to right: unfenced yard overgrown with weeds; paved area for unloading and loading freight for a commercial building; fenced-in backyard with unmowed grass, weeds, and trash; and a back street loading dock for a large bakery.

Fig. 1-3. A partial building consisting of only two walls (side and front) sits against a backdrop of the waterfront. Only the visible walls have been modeled—the rest of the structure is just bracing and sheet styrene.

like a large city fading up and off into the background. You can also place low-rise buildings in front of the street (i.e., between the viewer and the street) so viewers look over the building to see the pedestrians and vehicles in the street as well as other structures across the street. This gives viewers the impression that they are standing in the middle of a city. If the street is not parallel with the edge of the layout—if it slants toward the back, for instance—you'll want to place complete buildings on both sides of the street to add depth to the scene (see fig. 1-1). That way you can either look down the street or over buildings into the street as it slants away. Either view is effective in conveying the big city effect.

The big city effect is also more convincing when you position complete buildings in front of either a partial building or a flat, which may be part of a backdrop. By leaving a space between these structures, such as an alley or side street, you'll add depth to the scene.

Modeling the rear of a complete building, particularly if it is clearly visible, is as important as its front. The backs of commercial or residential buildings usually face alleys or backyards (see fig. 1-2). Industrial buildings have paved areas in the rear with loading docks for delivery trucks or possibly a railroad siding. As you'll see in Chapters 3 and 4, the detail you add to back walls and back

lots of your buildings goes a long way to enhance the character of your entire city scene.

Where to Use Partial Buildings

Partial buildings work best when only those walls that can be seen by the viewer need to exist (see fig. 1-3). It's common to use a partial building when a portion of it is close to a backdrop or when it is needed to fill a corner. In these cases you can't see a detailed rear wall, so there is no reason to model it. However, some form of bracing is necessary to

maintain the building's structural integrity. In addition, if the front of the building has windows, you will need to prevent the viewer from looking right through the building and out its open back. Simple sheet styrene across the back of the structure serves both purposes. For large partial buildings with big open backs, sheet styrene is expensive. In these cases you can brace the back with plastic structural shapes—such as those made by Plastruct and Evergreen—and paint the windows black from the inside. Wherever

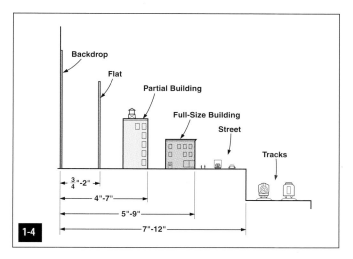

1-4

1-5

1-6

Fig. 1-4. Cross section through a cityscape showing the relative positioning (in inches) from the backdrop of the different city elements. The measurements are relative and can be larger to suit your layout.

Fig. 1-5. Full and partial buildings line the front of this cityscape. Two inches behind them are flats (building marked "Rooms") and an inch behind the flats are backdrop structures pasted onto the wall. Note the sense of depth you get, even though the scene is only 12 inches deep.

Fig. 1-6. Looking from a dark alley across a street to a flat made from the front of a building kit placed against a wall with a backdrop. The viewer does not see the alley end at the wall; rather, it intersects in a T with a street parallel to the wall.

possible, I make partial buildings from stock kits or modular building components. There are, however, times when a special shape or set of details require that I kitbash the structure using a combination of kit, modular, and scrap parts.

Where to Use Flats

A flat consists of one wall of a building—front, back, or side. While flats are usually printed on paper and pasted onto cardboard, they can also be plastic or urethane walls that are left over from building kits, or from modular building components.

There are a few ideal ways to use flats. In the first, the flat adds depth to a cityscape without great expense. When placed behind freestanding buildings (see fig. 1-4), its sides cannot be seen and are not required, which saves valuable space. Positioning the flat in front of the backdrop creates the illusion of depth and serves as a transition between the freestanding, three-dimensional structures in the foreground and the two-dimensional backdrop in the rear (see fig. 1-5).

Another way to use flats is at the end of a street that runs through the city and ends at the backdrop. You can glue the flat right onto the backdrop across all or part of the end of the street. If the flat runs completely across the end of the street, it gives the impression that the street turns to run parallel with the backdrop (see fig. 1-6). A third method is to cut printed buildings out of a commercial backdrop and glue them across only part of the street. This creates the illusion that the street goes over a hill and disappears down the other side at the backdrop

Where to Use a Backdrop

Backdrops are an integral part of a cityscape. For the purpose of a city scene, you'll want to create a backdrop that consists of pictures of distant buildings printed on paper; it will be mounted on a wall or vertical visual barrier at the back of the scene. Note that commercial backdrops include sky above the buildings. I've found that the top of the sky (i.e., the top of the backdrop) is too low for my layout. For example, most backdrops are 24″ high, and I've got basement walls that run anywhere from 36″ to 42″ from track level to the ceiling. I resolved the problem by painting the walls behind the layout light sky blue. Then I use a modeler's knife to cut the printed sky away from the backdrop buildings. I carefully paint the top edge of the remaining portion of the backdrop (the buildings) with the same blue used on the walls to hide the seam. After coating the back of the backdrop paper with spray adhesive, I

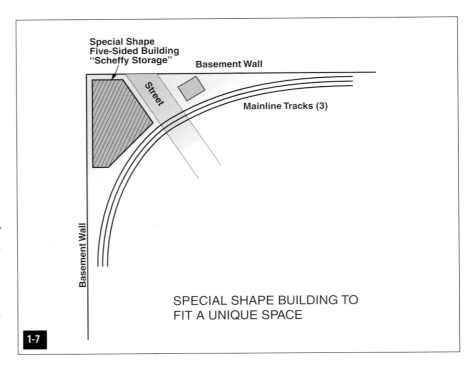

Fig. 1-7. Plan view of Scheffy Storage warehouse. The unique shape of this structure is dictated by the basement walls, mainline tracks, and a street. This example shows how a building's shape may be defined by the available space.

paste it directly onto the wall. The blue wall above the buildings makes an effective sky and allows you to mix backdrop buildings from a number of different vendors.

As shown in fig. 1-4, the most effective location of a backdrop is behind full buildings, partial buildings, and flats. Since the buildings in backdrops are printed smaller than full size, they look far away. I explain more about this illusion of distance in the section on *forced perspective*.

Backdrops also work well when tracks run along a wall. Gluing a backdrop on the wall gives the illusion that the railroad is part of the city. This may be the only option if your tracks are right next to a wall.

Special Buildings to Fit Special Spaces

Every layout has difficult-to-fill urban spaces such as corners or intersections between angled streets. You can fill these areas with complete or partial buildings. Unfortunately, most urban kits on the market are designed

to build rectangular structures, and oddly shaped spaces require either kitbashing or the use of modular building components. For small areas with simple shapes (triangles, parallelograms, etc.) I use kit parts and file, cut, or splice the parts to get the final shape. Figure 1-3 shows a good example of a triangular building that I made for the urban railroad module discussed in Chapter 4. I built the two visible walls of the structure from Design Preservation Models (DPM) modular building components and glued them at right angles to each other. The back of the building was open, and I covered it with sheet styrene to prevent viewers from looking through the building and seeing the basement wall.

For spaces with more complex shapes, you can build custom structures from modular building components. For example, my layout has a corner where three mainline tracks running along the walls curve through 90°, leaving a space between the tracks and the corner of the base-

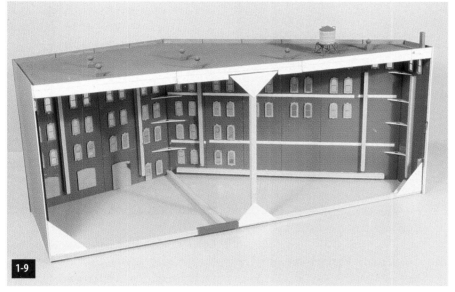

Fig. 1-8. This large warehouse was built with DPM Modular Building Components to fill a unique, five-sided space. The rear and right walls sit in a corner of the basement, while the remaining three front on the tracks or the street. Only those walls that could be seen by visitors were built from DPM modules.

Fig. 1-9. The rear of the warehouse is open and braced with plastic structural shapes and gussets. There is no need to waste DPM modules where they cannot be seen.

ment. To make matters worse, a street crosses the tracks near the middle of the curve and runs back at an angle into the corner. I filled this oddball space by building a five-sided, five-story-high warehouse from DPM modular building components. One wall ran alongside the street, a second was parallel to the curving tracks, and a third, very short wall ran from the tracks to the basement wall. The two back sides of the structure were against the walls of the basement and could not be seen (see fig. 1-7).

I made the shorter of these invisible sides from .020″ sheet styrene to fill the opening and left the longer side open, bracing it with Plastruct structural shapes. With the roof in place, the warehouse is rigid enough to be lifted in and out of its location. Pictures of the front of the structure and its open, braced rear appear in figs. 1-8 and 1-9. We will look further at the placement and function of this building as part of a cityscape in Chapter 2.

Forced Perspective

Fig. 1. This view from author's apartment in New York, taken in July 1961, looks north along Lexington Avenue. The church steeple referred to in the text (½ mile away) is the small spire in the center of the picture.

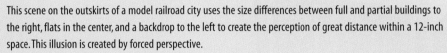

This scene on the outskirts of a model railroad city uses the size differences between full and partial buildings to the right, flats in the center, and a backdrop to the left to create the perception of great distance within a 12-inch space. This illusion is created by forced perspective.

Fig. 2. If we were to stand on the rooftop of a building in a model city, this is what we would see looking toward the city center a mile or two away. In reality, this scene is less than 12 inches deep, and the sense of distance is created by each row of buildings getting smaller: full building—flat—backdrop. This is forced perspective at work.

I grew up in the middle of New York City in the 1940s and 50s. From my ninth-floor apartment window, I could look north along the avenue over lower buildings. A few blocks away were two taller apartment houses, which looked small. A half mile beyond was a large church, whose high steeple looked tiny. At that distance, buses and trucks on the avenue were only colored dots (see fig. 1). From where I stood, New York looked like (and was) a very big city!

If I could duplicate that New York scene exactly in HO, it would take over 30 feet; yet most layouts have only 6″ to 18″ in depth for a city scene. Fortunately, there is a method you can use to trick your eye into thinking that buildings set only inches away are far off in the distance. This is a technique called *forced perspective*.

Forced perspective is the use of objects that are reduced in size to create the illusion of great distance in a very small space. A simple example is to model the scenery and buildings behind a train to a smaller scale than the train

itself. When the viewer looks over the train at the buildings, they appear to be far away because of their smaller size, even though only inches may separate the two. Your eye perceives these decreases in size as increased distance.

How to Create Forced Perspective

When using forced perspective, It's helpful to create a visual barrier between the railroad and the city. The most common way to do this is to place the cityscape 2 or more inches higher than tracks in the foreground. A retaining wall between the two levels works well and follows the prototypical practice of many railroads. Visually, you'll group the tracks in the foreground as one set of objects, all of the same general size, with their depth defined by the physical distance to the retaining wall. Then you'll look up and see the vertically separated cityscape as a second set of objects getting smaller and smaller. The smaller size enhances the illusion of distance through forced perspective.

Within a cityscape, the best way to achieve a sense of distance is to position the different elements of the city (full buildings, partial buildings, flats, and the backdrop), and then to reduce the physical size of each element the farther it is from the viewer. Using an HO layout as an example, the trains in the foreground (the closest objects to the viewer) are HO scale, or 1/87 actual size. In the cityscape, the complete buildings nearest the tracks are also HO scale. Ideally, partial build-

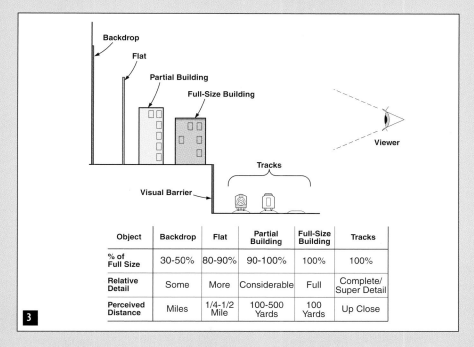

Object	Backdrop	Flat	Partial Building	Full-Size Building	Tracks
% of Full Size	30-50%	80-90%	90-100%	100%	100%
Relative Detail	Some	More	Considerable	Full	Complete/ Super Detail
Perceived Distance	Miles	1/4-1/2 Mile	100-500 Yards	100 Yards	Up Close

3

Fig. 3. As viewers look across a set of trains they encounter a visual barrier (the retaining wall) that separates a set of objects of one size (the trains) from a set of decreasing size (buildings, flats, and backdrop). The table at the bottom of the drawing shows the relationship between these objects in terms of percentage of full size, relative detail, and perceived distance.

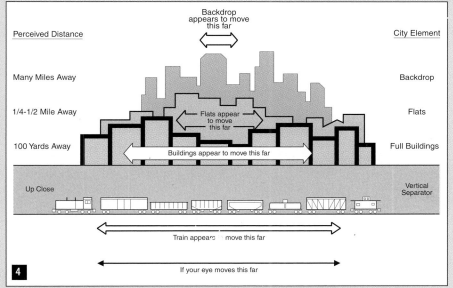

4

Fig. 4. As long as there is a space, even if it is only inches, between the objects in a cityscape (full buildings, flats, and backdrop), they will appear to move at different rates of speed as the viewers observe them.

buildings, flats, and the backdrop, and the sense of distance they convey through forced perspective.

Fortunately, the manufacturers of flats and backdrops make their products with forced perspective in mind. Walthers Instant Buildings flats, for example, average 20 to 25 percent smaller than full-size HO. Similarly, the closest buildings in the city backdrops of Walthers, Detail Associates, and other manufacturers are about half HO scale (about 45 percent smaller, on the average), while those in the distance are even smaller.

Relative Motion

A second and more subtle way to apply forced perspective is through the relative motion of near and distant structures. If you travel through a city by rail or road, look out the window and take a minute to notice how the buildings appear to move past you. Those closest go by at the speed you are moving. Structures two to three blocks away seem to move much more slowly, while buildings many blocks (or miles) in the distance appear to stand still.

Properly placed, buildings, flats, and a backdrop on your cityscape can achieve the same effect (see fig. 4). While the difference in speed is much smaller than in the prototype, it is noticeable, and helps contribute to the sense of distance in the setting.

ings, if they are immediately behind the complete buildings, would be smaller by about 10 percent to make them appear farther away. However, since partial structures are made from standard kits or modular components, a 10 percent reduction in size is hard to achieve. The next layer back consists of flats, about 4″ to 7″ behind the front line of buildings. I find that making flats 20 to 30 percent smaller than HO makes them look much far-

ther away. In the backdrop, usually 6″ to 12″ back, reducing the size of the closest structures to 50 percent of HO scale makes them appear even farther away than the flats. Other buildings in the backdrop should be even smaller, perhaps 60 to 70 percent of HO. Why? Because to the eye, small size equals distance; the smaller the building the farther away it seems (see fig. 2). Figure 3 shows the relative sizes between complete buildings, partial

A cityscape makes an effective backdrop behind an urban station or yard. If it consists of the right elements (buildings, flats, and backdrop) and employs forced perspective, the cityscape backdrop makes the yard operator and other viewers feel that they are right in a large city.

BUILDING A CITY
CHAPTER 2

The City
As a
Backdrop

There are three basic ways to build a city backdrop: use a printed backdrop and flats, build a three-dimensional cityscape, or construct functional buildings that integrate the three-dimensional approach with a specific purpose (i.e., hiding staging tracks). Depending on your layout, you can use these techniques singly or in combination.

Fig. 2-1. An Alco RS-1 heading a short freight rumbles through the outskirts of a city. Even though the city is only a backdrop and flats, it still adds an urban feeling to the railroad.

Fig. 2-2. This Boston & Maine switcher is moving a string of cars through a cut in a city. The urban backdrop and flats on the wall to the left, along with the factory buildings on the right, make it look as if the city surrounds the cut.

Building a "Printed City" – Backdrop and Flats

The simplest type of city backdrop is a commercially printed, paper backdrop glued to a wall behind your railroad. Printed city backdrops are most useful when trackwork runs right next to a wall (see fig. 2-1). The backdrop gives the illusion of the city fading into the distance. By placing some small bushes or a low fence between the tracks and the printed backdrop you can visually isolate the full-size trains from the half-size printed buildings. You can also use a backdrop as a transition from an urban to a rural setting by adding more bushes and some green groundcover around the tracks as the backdrop turns into country.

While very easy to construct and effective for short distances of 2 to 3 feet, the printed backdrop has two limitations. Printed backdrops have no "depth" other than the printed perspective and shadows in the artwork. And because backdrop buildings are printed at 40 to 50 percent of full size, they're not very convincing if you place them just behind the tracks, especially if the shadow of a passing train is visible on the backdrop.

I find that combining flats with a backdrop greatly enhances its effectiveness. I usually locate the flats (sized about 80 to 90 percent of full scale) along the center of the city backdrop with printed backdrops on the ends (see fig. 2-3). With the backdrop on each end you can create the illusion of the city fading into the distance and achieve an excellent transition between urban and rural scenery. The flats in the middle appear to be full-size buildings next to the tracks, so that the railroad looks as if it is in the heart of the city. You can glue buildings cut out of a backdrop to the wall above or between individual flats to create an additional sense of depth. You can also use walls from city structure kits as flats to provide the three-dimensional effect. If space permits, you could also position a very shallow partial building within the flats to further enhance this effect (see fig. 2-2).

To construct a printed city, you'll want to start by painting the background (basement walls, view block, etc.) a light sky blue. Next, cut out the city (or country) portion of a commercial backdrop and discard the printed sky. This allows you to use backdrops from different manufacturers without worrying about whether the sky or cloud colors match. Use a pencil to mark the intended backdrop location on the wall. Mark only a few key points (ends, high points, etc.), as you will have to remove the pencil marks once the backdrop is installed. Lay the backdrop face down on a piece of newspaper and apply a coat of spray adhesive such as 3M Super 77, available at most hardware and art supply stores. Carefully pick the backdrop up by the edges, and place it on the wall so that its center bonds first. Gently smooth the backdrop from the center towards the edges to get an even bond and eliminate trapped air bubbles. This takes a bit of practice, and you should try a few dry runs using scrap paper on a piece of plywood to get the technique down pat.

Wherever possible, I also like to add freestanding flats $1/4''$ to $1/2''$ away from a backdrop to add a three-dimensional effect. Start by gluing the flat on a piece of cardboard with spray adhesive to give it some structural rigidity. Then cut the flat and cardboard along the outline of the printed buildings with a hobby knife. If the edges of the cardboard are too light and stand out, you might need to run a black or brown marking pen over the edges to hide the stark color of the cardboard. Also be sure to glue a few pieces of $1/4''$ square scale wood across the back of the cardboard to keep it from warping. This is important if your pike is in a basement where the air is damp in the summer.

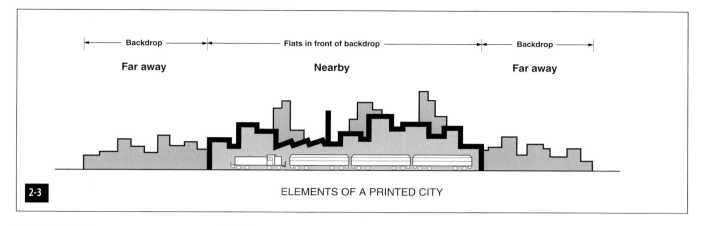

Backdrop — Flats in front of backdrop — Backdrop

Far away   **Nearby**   **Far away**

2-3   ELEMENTS OF A PRINTED CITY

Fig. 2-3. This figure shows the placement of backdrop and flats, both mounted on a wall. Their relative sizes give the illusion that the center portion of the city is nearer to the viewer than the ends.

Fig. 2-4. Although it measures only 22″ x 48″, Bob and Bev Shea's module conveys the urban clutter of buildings and streets very effectively.

Be careful not to leave too much space between the flat and wall (½″ is a practical maximum) so the flat cannot cast unrealistic shadows on the backdrop. Finally, apply contact glue to the wood strips and mount the flat on the backdrop or wall.

While a printed backdrop and flats may not be as dramatic as a three-dimensional cityscape, they can be very effective if you have limited space.

The Three-Dimensional Backdrop

The most realistic kind of city backdrop consists of three-dimensional buildings (including streets, vehicles, and people), flats, and a printed backdrop. While the 10″ to 12″ of space between the wall and your railroad this option requires is more than you'll need for a printed

city, you can make the most of this area if you follow some important guidelines:

• Draw a working plan of the area you want to model.

• Build your cityscape above any trackwork in the foreground, even if by only a few inches. This creates the visual barrier between the railroad and the city.

• Place three-dimensional buildings in the foreground, with flats towards the rear, and a printed backdrop on a wall or divider.

• Angle streets away from the front of the layout—angled streets are longer than those running straight into the wall, and their ends can be disguised by flats.

• Do not run a street along the front of the cityscape, parallel to the tracks, for the entire length of your city. It should turn and angle back

into the city at a point ½ to ⅔ the length of the cityscape.

Let's look at an example of a three-dimensional cityscape backdrop that demonstrates how all the above guidelines can work to create an effective scene.

Though originally designed as a portable HO module, the Sheas' city is now being built into their home layout. The cityscape measures 4′ long by 22″ deep and sits 2″ above and behind a two-track main line (see fig. 2-4). The tracks are 6″ behind the edge of the layout, so that two to three structures can be placed between viewers and the main line. This adds realism and the illusion that the railroad is running through the city. Immediately behind the tracks is a 2″ high cut-stone retaining wall, which serves as the visual barrier between the tracks and the city. A light blue piece of plywood serves as the sky behind the city.

Both the main line and cityscape backdrop rest on a benchwork frame covered with ½″ plywood. A 2″ thick piece of extruded polystyrene insulation, set behind the main line, raises

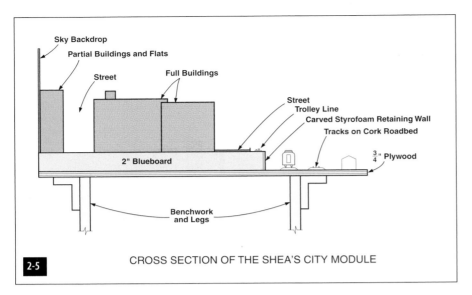

Sky Backdrop
Partial Buildings and Flats
Street
Full Buildings
Street
Trolley Line
Carved Styrofoam Retaining Wall
Tracks on Cork Roadbed
2" Blueboard
¾" Plywood
Benchwork and Legs

2-5 CROSS SECTION OF THE SHEA'S CITY MODULE

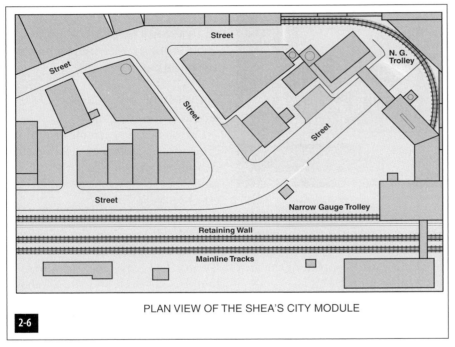

Street
Street
Street
Street
Street
N. G. Trolley
Street
Narrow Gauge Trolley
Retaining Wall
Mainline Tracks

2-6 PLAN VIEW OF THE SHEA'S CITY MODULE

Fig. 2-5. Section through the Sheas' module, showing the relative positioning of tracks and city structures.

Fig. 2-6. Plan of the Shea's city module, showing location of streets, tracks, and all major buildings. Note the angles of the streets with respect to the front of the module.

the cityscape and serves as a light-weight base for the streets and buildings. A cross section through the cityscape is shown in fig. 2-5.

After installing the track and insulation board, Bob and Bev made a detailed, full-scale plan of the city by cutting a piece of cardboard to the same size as the raised cityscape and drawing in the outlines of streets and blocks (see fig. 2-6). A main street runs along the front of the cityscape for two-thirds of its length and then turns and angles back into the city. A second street angles back (in the opposite direction) from an intersection with the first. By angling the streets, they look much longer than the 22" depth of the city. (see fig. 2-7).

Bev also made use of three-dimensional, cardboard building mockups and moved them around the cardboard street plan until the city had the right look. In general, lower buildings are placed at the front of the cityscape and higher ones towards the rear. When the design was complete, she then transferred it

onto the insulation board. You'll find that making cardboard mockups is an easy way to see what your final cityscape will look like before you build a number of kits and find they don't fit.

The next area to construct are streets and sidewalks. The Sheas set their city in New England at the end of the 1930s, a time when older cobblestone streets were repaved with asphalt. However, heavy city traffic and winter weather causes the new paving to wear away in patches to expose cobbles below. You can create this effect by outlining each street with .020" sheet styrene and gluing it to the surface of the cityscape. Next, glue pieces of Kibri no. 4124 plastic cobblestone sheet in the street where the cobbles will show through. Then spread wall-joint compound (spackle) between the styrene street sides and smooth it with a piece of wood to form the pavement (see fig. 2-8). The compound covers only the edges of the pieces of cobblestone. As it dries, the compound cracks in natural patterns. You can enlarge these cracks with the back of a no. 11 blade in a hobby knife to make them more visible. You'll want to paint the street surfaces with Floquil Grimy Black with a little white added, and smudge in oil stains with charcoal. And finally, add N gauge sand in the wider cracks and secure it with Woodland Scenics Scenic Cement.

The cut stone retaining wall at the front of the cityscape comes from a piece of white insulation board (Styrofoam) with the grooves between the granite blocks carved into the surface with a hobby knife. The

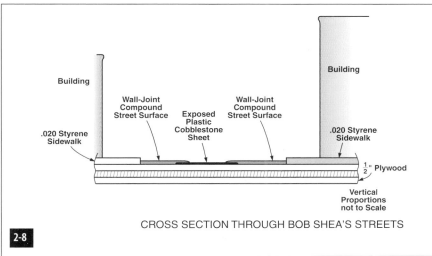

Fig. 2-7. When looking down one of the streets on the module, you get the impression that it runs a long way into the city and curves around buildings in the distance. The street slants into the module and therefore looks much longer than the actual depth of the module.

Fig. 2-8. Cross section through a street on the Sheas' module, showing how old cobblestone pavement was made to "show through" the asphalt road surfaces.

Fig. 2-9. A close look at the street detail reveals spots where old cobblestones have appeared as the newer asphalt has worn away. Note the cracks and discoloration in the pavement from passing cars and trucks.

wall has a base coat of Concrete paint with a finger-painted coat of roof brown applied over it. Dry-brushed shades of Grimy Black and Rust also help pick out highlights and make the completed wall look even more realistic. Drainpipes, made from pieces of copper tubing inserted into the wall, also improve the appearance.

Now it's on to the building construction. As in most New England cities in the 1930s, brick structures predominate, with a few art-deco and iron-front structures. The Sheas used commercial kits from City Classics, Design Preservation Models (DPM), and Walthers for the majority of the structures, modifying them if necessary to fit the scene. For example, by carving doors into the front of DPM's Carr's Auto Parts, they created a firehouse (see fig. 2-10). Where no kit is available for a

Fig. 2-10. You'd never know that this firehouse started life as a kit for a plumbing supply shop. By cutting doors, giving it a "municipal" paint job, and putting clean, ready-to-go, red fire engines in the driveway, Bob Shea has demonstrated how effective kitbashing urban buildings can be.

Fig. 2-11. New England mill buildings are distinguished by their red brick facades, tall chimneys, and corrugated-iron walkways between buildings. The Harwood Furniture complex at one end of the city module makes you feel as though you're standing in the middle of a classic mill city.

building, you could also use DPM Building Modules to create a custom structure. An example is a complex of New England mill buildings on one side of the cityscape (see fig. 2-11). The Sheas made corrugated iron bridges connecting the mill structures and the peaked iron roof for one building of the mill from Evergreen corrugated styrene sheet. They used Grandt Line windows in the bridges. Since the city is viewed from the front, the Sheas made the back walls of most buildings of sheet styrene painted the same color as the rest of the structure. They used the leftover parts to kitbash and add to other buildings.

Just as the Sheas have, you can add window shades to your structures using pieces of colored envelope glued to the acetate windows at different heights. For the storefronts you might consider using printed windows made

by Main Street Graphics to give the street a commercial look.

It's important to use a variety of colors to differentiate the large number of brick buildings. A light wash made from diluted Polly Scale Concrete and a dark wash made from diluted india ink added over the structures help further differentiate the colors. Pastel chalks are also useful for weathering the buildings and pulling out unique details. Finally, don't neglect to add building details, including wall and roof signs and advertisements, roof surfaces and fixtures, and window details. You can read more about colors and wash mixes, as well as building details, in Chapter 5.

City streets need detail. Since their city depicts the late 1930s, the Sheas chose vehicles from Wheel Works, Jordan Products, and Busch—these companies make a variety of vehicles from the 1920s and '30s. You can modify some of these car and truck kits by placing different bodies on the chassis and adding open doors and even drivers to a few of the cars. You could even repaint vehicles to match colors you find in old magazine advertisements and postcards. Cast ornate lampposts from Woodland Scenics are typical of the wrought-iron styles used in the 1920s and '30s; and other street details, including fire hydrants, mail boxes, and fire alarm boxes, are available to com-

plete a scene set in practically any era.

To populate the city, the Sheas painted bare Preiser figures using acrylics in appropriate clothing colors for the 1930s. Then he used the same techniques I described in an article, "Populate Your Layout," which appeared in the March 1998 edition of *Model Railroader* magazine. Figure 2-12 shows the street details, vehicles, and people.

As a final step, fig. 2-13 shows how flats from the front walls of taller structures can be glued to a sky backdrop at the ends of the streets to create a desirable effect. These, combined with the angled street layout, can make a boulevard look much longer than the actual depth of the cityscape.

The Sheas' city is an excellent example of the realism of a three-dimensional city backdrop. While the plan, number of buildings, and amount of detail will vary to suit your taste, this type of city backdrop best conveys the look and feel of a real city behind the tracks.

The Functional City Backdrop

A third kind of city backdrop is one that serves a specific function in addition to giving the illusion of a large city in the background. With this type of design you're able to disguise trackwork (main line, yard, or staging area) in and under a cityscape that is behind an urban terminal or

Fig. 2-12. The streets of the module are well detailed, from the title on the windows of the Seaman's Bank, to the vehicles and people on the streets, to the urban "hardware" like streetlights and mailboxes. These details make this module come alive and feel like a real city.

Fig. 2-13. As the viewer peers down the main street, it looks like a long way before the street curves off to the left in the distance. Slanting the street away from the front of the module gives it extra length, and a line of flats made from tall building fronts that stretch across the end of the street at the rear makes it appear to curve to the left.

yard. Unlike the previous example, it's not practical to have streets running into a cityscape whose function is to hide tracks—those streets would have to cross the hidden tracks, giving away their existence. Therefore, the buildings in this kind of cityscape must sit side by side with no gaps between them. While this may seem unrealistic, if you choose buildings of different heights and architectures to break up the cityscape, you will hardly notice the lack of streets (see lead photo). In addition, the windows of each structure must be opaque so that trains moving behind them cannot be seen. Finally, you also need to modify the construction of the buildings so the trains can literally run through them.

One of the main stations on my layout represents New Haven, Connecticut—once the hub of the New York, New Haven & Hartford Railroad, which I model. The terminal and its yard measure 12' long by 28" wide and are located along a wall of my basement. Immediately behind and approximately 6" above the yard, against the wall, is a three-track main line that climbs a 1 percent grade (see fig. 2-14). While the main line is an essential part of my layout, its location is unrealistic and would rarely be found in real life. Therefore, I decided to hide the line by building the city of New Haven around it. I wanted to look above the terminal yard to a city backdrop without seeing the three-track main line. The space for the cityscape measured only 10" deep, and its structures had to be built in front of and over the hidden tracks. This meant that I had to cut away the sides of each structure so that trains could run through them (see fig. 2-15). As I mentioned earlier, each building had to be directly adjacent those on either side of it. All windows had to be blacked out so that trains on the hidden main line could not be seen. Behind the three-dimensional buildings I needed flats mounted $1/4$" to $1/2$" in front of the wall, as well as paper buildings, cut out of a backdrop and glued to the wall itself. These two layers add depth and forced perspective to my cityscape. While my task was to hide a main line, you can use a similar technique to bury a staging area, holding yard, or other portion of your layout that you do not want people to see.

The first step is to determine how to support this type of cityscape. I decided to build a narrow shelf, made from $1/8$" Masonite, to support the front of the buildings and the top of the retaining wall behind the yard. Since the shelf had to be level while the main line rose at a 1 percent grade, I used pieces of stripwood to shim the Masonite until it was level (see fig. 2-16).

The next step is to decide what buildings to use for the cityscape. I needed commercial kits that when placed side by side measured the same length as the hidden main line. The structures had to have different architectural styles so that a visitor's eyes would notice the buildings, not the lack of streets or spaces between them. I also wanted to match the kind of structures found around the prototype New Haven station in 1948 (the period that I model). With all of these criteria in mind, I chose the following (see fig. 2-14):

• Three buildings (Powerhouse, NE Screw Machine Building, Beer Building) made from portions of a Heljan brewery, which I had bought in the 1970s as a supply of parts for urban modeling.

• A $6^1/2$" long three-story, cardboard brownstone (Apartment House). This kit is no longer made, but similar buildings are available from

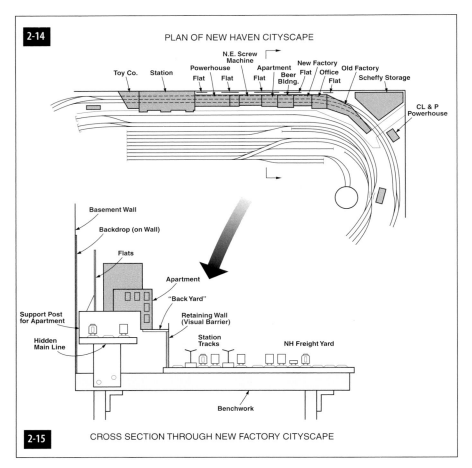

2-14

PLAN OF NEW HAVEN CITYSCAPE

Toy Co.　Station　Powerhouse Flat　Flat　N.E. Screw Machine Flat　Apartment Beer Bldng.　New Factory Flat　Office Flat　Old Factory Scheffy Storage

CL & P Powerhouse

Basement Wall

Backdrop (on Wall)

Flats

Apartment

"Back Yard"

Support Post for Apartment

Retaining Wall (Visual Barrier)

Hidden Main Line

Station Tracks

NH Freight Yard

Benchwork

2-15

CROSS SECTION THROUGH NEW FACTORY CITYSCAPE

Fig. 2-14. Plan of New Haven yard, showing the main line behind it, which is hidden under the cityscape.

Fig. 2-15. Section through New Haven yard, showing the relative elevations of the yard, cityscape, and hidden main line under the city.

the pen line and sprinkling Woodland Scenics weed foam onto the wet paint. Once the paint dries and you brush off the excess foam, the result is quite realistic (see fig. 2-17).

The Apartment and Beer Building also shared a backyard, but like the apartments in many cities, this one is dirt overgrown with weeds. To re-create this type of yard, you can paint the shelf Polly Scale Earth and sprinkle a mixture of soil, earth, burnt grass, and weed fine foam onto the wet paint. When it's dry, add a layer of burnt and green grass coarse foam and seal it with Woodland Scenics Scenic Cement. You should also add a piece of Central Valley board fence across each end of the yard (see fig. 2-17). I will cover painting this fence later on in this section.

On my layout I needed to design a corner where the main line curves to run under the cityscape. I made a road running from the wall of the basement, across the main line to the Old Factory that serves two purposes: first as a visual boundary between the city and surrounding landscape, and second as access to the old factory. On one side of the road I placed the CL&P Powerhouse, which I built from a Kibri Kit. I built a large five-story warehouse, the Scheffy Storage Co., from DPM Modules (see figs. 1-8 and 1-9 in Chapter 1) on the other side of the road.

A road running dead into a blank wall doesn't make for a very realistic scene. You can easily achieve the illusion that the road goes over a hill and curves away in the distance (see fig. 2-18). Start by gluing a four-story building flat on the wall slightly overlapping the left lane, and a second,

International Hobbies Corp. (IHC).
• The Roberts Printing Co. from Walthers, a reinforced concrete, four-story building with brick curtain walls and one vertical line of windows cut out of the front of the structure (New Factory).
• A four-story brick (Office) building made from DPM Modules with Victorian Sash. A Kibri factory three stories high with many industrial roof and wall fittings (Old Factory). This last building was in the corner, where the main line went around a 90° curve, so I spliced the front and back of the kit together at a slight angle to give the building a concave shape. This structure helped hide where the main line goes under the cityscape—more on that later.

Be sure that you lay the front wall of each building side by side along the main line to see if they fit. My walls were off by about an inch, so I added a one-story, 1" long wall to

one end of the Apartment to make the total cityscape the right length. Since there are no streets running into my city, the walls facing the New Haven terminal become the rear of each building, and the Masonite shelf serves as their backyards. You'll want to mark the end of each building on the shelf to denote each yard and glue pieces of 1/8" square wood along the shelf to align the wall of each building. These strips are important, as all of the buildings have to be removable to access the hidden tracks.

I then painted the backyards on the shelf. My powerhouse and Screw Machine Co. share a cracked concrete yard painted Polly Scale Aged Concrete with 6' square concrete blocks and cracks outlined with a fine black marking pen. You could have weeds growing up through the cracks and between blocks by painting a fine line of Aged Concrete over

2-16

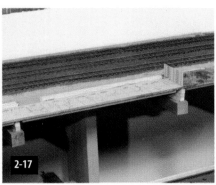

2-17

Fig. 2-16. New Haven Yard and mainline benchwork before construction of the cityscape. The shelf supporting the cityscape has been glued to the 1″ x 1″ pieces of wood protruding from the mainline roadbed supports. Though the main line rises at a 1 percent grade, the cityscape shelf will remain level through the use of shims.

Fig. 2-17. Closeup of the cityscape support shelf in place. The concrete backyard with weed-filled cracks on the left and the weed-filled backyard on the right will be behind different buildings. Also note the shims on top of the supports to keep the shelf level.

shorter flat in line with the right side-walk. Then cut two buildings from a paper backdrop, each of which consists of an end wall with the front of the structure on its right-hand side. In addition, each roof should slant down and away in perspective. Glue the first of these so that its front overlaps two-thirds of the right lane of the road and its roof falls between the first and second story of the flat. Then glue the second over the first so that its front overlaps about one-third of the right lane and its roof is just above the second story of the flat.

Before installing any buildings in the cityscape, you'll want to build a retaining wall, as I did, to fill the vertical space between the New Haven yard and the cityscape (see fig. 2-19). The top of my wall is level with the surface of the backyards. I made the wall from ⅛″ Masonite covered with embossed cut-stone paper (Faller no. 604). By gluing a narrow vertical strip of the stone paper, with its edges painted brown, across the gap where each piece of stone paper met, you can effectively hide the joint with a decorative stone pilaster. In order to have accessible wiring, make all wall sections removable by seating their bases in between ³⁄₃₂″ square pieces of wood glued to the surface of the yard and securing their tops with no. 1 wood screws to ¼″ square wood glued under the backyard shelf. Be sure to paint the heads of the screws dark brown to blend in with the color of the wall.

Installing fences along the top of the wall running the length of each backyard prevents the city population from falling over the edge. I used Plastruct chain-link fence and Central Valley wood fencing. The

2-18

2-19

2-20

Fig. 2-18. The factory road, which actually dead-ends at the basement wall, appears to go over a hill curving to the right. The illusion is achieved by the two backdrop buildings on the right. One is low and to the right; the other, glued over it, is higher and slightly to the left.

Fig. 2-19. A stone retaining wall hides the benchwork supporting the hidden main line and serves as a foundation for the future New Haven cityscape.

Fig. 2-20. Two kinds of fence top the retaining wall: a chain-link industrial fence on the right, and a wooden board fence on the left. Washes of diluted india ink applied individually bring out the grain of the boards and differentiate them from each other.

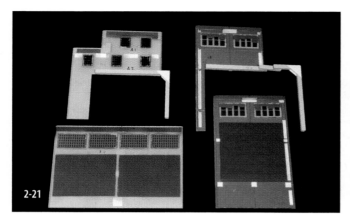

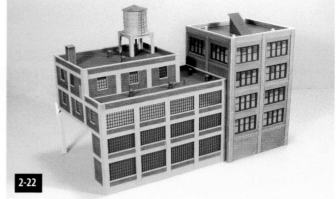

Fig. 2-21. This view of the insides of the end and front walls of the New Factory and Office buildings shows the plastic beams on the end pieces. These will span the tracks of the hidden main line. The black paper glued over the front windows of the structures hides the headlights of trains on the hidden main line.

Fig. 2-22. Here's a front view of the assembled New Factory and Office buildings. Gluing the structures together prevents the viewer from seeing the hidden main line through a gap between them.

Fig. 2-23. Rear view of the assembled buildings, showing the plastic cross beams and rear support legs. The main line will pass through the opening beneath these beams.

Central Valley fence is plastic with excellent wood grain molded into it. Painting the fence Polly Scale Earth and brushing each board with one or more washes of diluted india ink (one part of ink to 30 parts of alcohol) brings out the wood grain and differentiates the board it from its neighbors (see fig. 2-20).

The next step is to construct each building in the cityscape. On my layout, these and all of the other structures have to span the three-track main line that tunnels through them. Consequently, they have no lower side walls. To support the structures' upper sides, which are visible, I used 1/4" square plastic structural shapes as cross beams over the mainline tracks. These beams extend from the front of the structure to the back edge of the mainline benchwork. Gluing triangular gussets cut from .015" styrene sheet to the leg joint helps strengthen the structure. You can completely hide all trains running on the main line by gluing black con-

struction paper over the back of the lower front windows in each building. Figure 2-21 shows the rear of the sides and front walls of the New Factory and Office so that you can see the cross beams, legs, and blacked-out windows.

In some cases buildings may fill the space better if they are assembled as a single unit. Build this type of structure by gluing the front, sides, back, and roof together to form each building's shell. Then cement the common walls (between the buildings) to each other, making sure that the bottom of the building fronts are level (see fig. 2-22). The rear of the two structures rests on the support legs (see fig. 2-23). I placed my buildings on the backyard shelf and adjusted the height with shims of .020" styrene under the legs until they were level. Be sure to check clearance between the building fronts and rear legs by running a train up the main line (see fig. 2-24).

As you can see in fig. 2-25, the

main line of my layout disappears between the Storage and Old Factory buildings, and its entry under the cityscape is well concealed. I placed the large Scheffy Storage building behind the tracks on the left side of the corner road, and put the CL&P Powerhouse on its right side. I then installed the Old Factory next to the Office in front of the tracks. I added the illusion that the main line really ran straight at an angle into the backdrop by making the roof of the Old Factory parallel to the Storage building. In reality (see fig. 2-26), the roof extends over the curving tracks, while the sheet styrene back of the Old Factory curves with the tracks under the roof. You can use a similar technique to hide the routing of tracks under buildings on your layout.

Building by building, I went on to add the rest of the structures over the main line, making sure that moving trains could not be seen through the cracks. If this does occur, install a

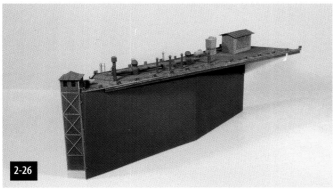

Fig. 2-24. The New Factory and Office buildings are in their final places over the main line with a train moving under them to test clearances.

Fig. 2-25. The completed corner, with Scheffy Storage behind the main line and the Old Factory in front of it. The tracks enter the cityscape by passing between two buildings, so there is no visible tunnel portal.

Fig. 2-26. Rear view of the Old Factory, showing the straight back line of the roof, and the false rear wall that curves with the tracks under the building. The straight back roof line gives the illusion that the main line angles into the wall/backdrop, even though it actually curves under the structure and into the cityscape.

Fig. 2-27. The Beer Building joins the cityscape next to the New Factory/Office structures. In addition, small buildings cut out of a backdrop and glued to the wall fill the gap between the three-dimensional structures. The small size of these buildings gives the illusion of a large city behind the front structures and adds depth and perspective to the cityscape.

baffle, made from .015″ sheet styrene. Attach the baffle to one building and extend it across the gap behind its neighbor.

Once the buildings are in place, you should note where too much wall (the "sky") is visible behind the lower buildings. After you mark (lightly) the wall where the sky appears, you'll want to remove the structure from the scene. Then, cut out groups of buildings from a Walthers city backdrop and mount them with spray adhesive on the wall. Add some brown paint below the backdrop buildings so they don't appear to be floating in the sky if a tall visitor should stand on tiptoe and look *down* behind the cityscape. In fig. 2-27 you can see some of these backdrop buildings just to the left of the Beer Building. I also added flats just behind the three-dimensional cityscape buildings to give a further feeling of depth. The flats are mounted on cardboard and braced with ¼″ square wood to keep them from warping. By gluing them to the rear legs of the cityscape buildings (which placed them ¼″ to ½″ off the wall) I added forced perspective to the cityscape, as described in Chapter 1. The completed New Haven cityscape—three-dimensional buildings, flats, and backdrop, all hiding a three-track main line—is shown in the lead photo. There's no doubt that your cityscape will turn out just as well.

In the next chapter, we'll look at a very different way of building a city by constructing a small, highly detailed, freestanding module. This takes less space than a long backdrop, can be viewed from all sides, and still gives the illusion that your railroad runs through a big city.

A city module, or small slice of a city, can be an effective way to make a model railroad appear to be passing through an urban environment. When combined with tracks running in a cut bridged by city streets, the city module is an excellent transition between rural surroundings and a city terminal.

BUILDING A CITY
CHAPTER 3

The City
As a
Scenic Module

Cities are large, and most layouts do not have the space to model even a portion of one. A city module allows you to build just enough of a city to create the illusion that your railroad runs through urban surroundings. The module can be one or two city blocks that are a part of your layout's local scenery (just as a hill is beside a main line). The city module stands alone and can be seen from all sides, including the fronts, sides, and back lots of buildings. It can also serve a specific function, such as the transition from a rural main line to an urban terminal and yard. However, unlike a prototype railroad, which runs through miles of suburbs to reach a city terminal, the city module can foreshorten this transition to a few feet. Placing the module in a restricted space, such as a corner, can be particularly effective.

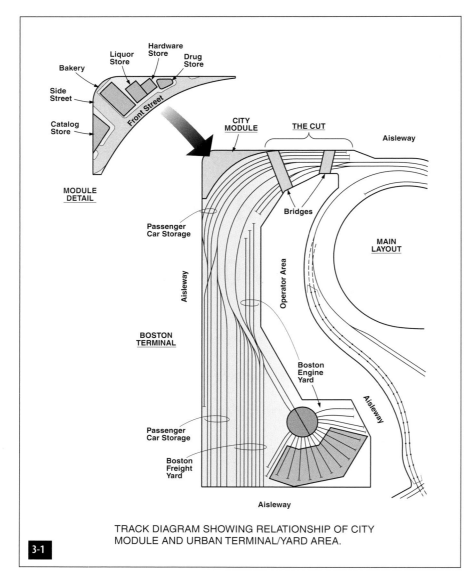

MODULE
DETAIL

TRACK DIAGRAM SHOWING RELATIONSHIP OF CITY
MODULE AND URBAN TERMINAL/YARD AREA.

3-1

Fig. 3-1. Track diagram showing the relationship of the city module to the main layout and urban terminal/yard area. In the upper left is a blow-up plan of the module with buildings and streets.

Fig. 3-2. This is the way my layout looked before the construction of the Boston city module. There was no visual transition between the main layout (in the foreground) and the South Station terminal and yard around the curve in the background.

based on Boston's South Station. A two-track main line leaves the main layout and enters the approach to the Boston yard. Here, it splits into separate, parallel leads to the terminal, a yard, and an engine facility. These leads swing around a 90° curve, at the end of which are the station's throat, the yard ladder, and the turntable and diesel storage tracks. Viewers can look at this curve from the outside of the layout or from an inside aisleway where the terminal control panel is located.

Like many other urban railroads, the main line to South Station was built through Boston in a stone-lined cut with the local streets passing over it on bridges. The right-of-way was shared by the New Haven and Boston & Albany railroads until 1968; and is now used by Amtrak, Commuter Rail, and Rapid Transit lines. The module also serves as a visual transition between rural and urban surroundings.

Even though my city module is only 3 feet long, it creates an illusion of the prototype's long cut through Boston and gives the viewer the look and feel of the real thing. The module consists of the following elements:

• A wall of the cut running along the outside edge of the benchwork leading to the curve into the yard.

• Two street bridges over the cut to help make it a transitional "gateway" to South Station.

• A city module—streets, buildings, vehicles, and pedestrians, built

3-2

Positioning the City Module

While the size, shape and contents of a city module should be designed to fit your layout, in this chapter we will look at a module on an outside corner of the layout, as shown in fig. 3-1.

The trackwork in this example is

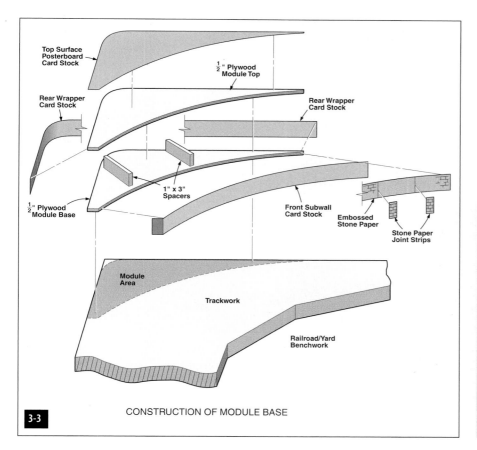

Fig. 3-3. Exploded view showing the construction of the module's base.

Fig. 3-4. This view of the mainline curve looking from the terminal toward the main layout (out of view at right) shows the installed city module base. Embossed stone paper covers the front of the module and will continue into the cut to be built next to it. The anchor for the first street bridge over the cut is visible on the inside edge of the benchwork at right in the picture.

Fig. 3-5. This view shows the outer wall of the cut, added outside the tracks, as well as the anchor for the second bridge over the cut. The main layout is visible at far right in the photo.

Fig. 3-6. Closeup of the completed anchor for the first bridge over the cut. The foamcore anchor, covered with embossed stone paper, matches the wall of the cut. The rectangular piece of wood between the tracks is a footing for one of the bridge's support piers.

above track level on the corner behind the curve—depicting a small slice of South Boston.

Building a Foundation for the City Module

The first step in building my city module was to construct a raised platform to fill the outer corner of the terminal benchwork and serve as its foundation (see fig. 3-2). You can fabricate this platform from two pieces of ½" plywood with 1" x 3" spacers glued between them, as shown in fig. 3-3. For my layout, this placed the top 3⅞" above track level, the same as the cut.

The 3⅞" dimension allows the highest piece of HO scale rolling stock on the layout to pass under the bridges I'll build across the cut. Also, be sure to round the outer corner of the platform so that viewers or operators don't catch their clothing on a sharp edge. The module base, seen in fig. 3-3, comprises various layers of plywood and cardboard.

For my module, I cut a piece of cardboard, the same shape as the top of the platform, and glued it to the plywood to form the surface of the module's streets. I painted the entire top surface of the module Floquil Grimy Black, a color similar to the

asphalt in Boston. To disguise the base of my module, I glued Faller no. 604 embossed stone paper, a close match to the prototype, to the curved inside wall of the cut above the trackwork. A number of manufacturers make similar embossed paper and plastic stonework with enough selection to match your taste (see Appendix). The paper versions are printed in color and achieve a realistic three-dimensional effect through printed shadows on the stonework and the embossing. The plastic versions have deeper embossing, but they are molded in either clear or gray plastic, which requires painting and highlighting.

When working with this stone paper, you can easily hide any joints by gluing a vertical strip of stone paper, 1/2″ wide, across the gap between each piece. You can also hide the exposed edges by using a brown pen to mark the white edges of the stone paper. To finish off my model, I glued a strip of 1/8″ square stripwood along the edge of the street above the cut wall to support a fence to be installed later (see fig. 3-3). The completed module base easily attaches to the benchwork with wood screws started from underneath the layout.

On my module, the tracks between the point where the main line to Boston branches off the main layout and the corner-mounted module are located in a cut, the same as the prototype. Since this trackwork contains switches, I built only the outer wall of the cut and left the inside open to reach derailments and perform track maintenance. As you see in fig. 3-5, a strip of 1/8″ Masonite forms the back wall of the cut.

You can easily add visual length to a cut by adding street bridges that span the track. Start by building abutments made from 1/4″ foamcore covered with stone paper at each end of the bridge. One abutment is glued to the wall of the cut; the other is sandwiched with a second piece of foamcore and left as a freestanding anchor (see fig. 3-6).

Be sure to set the tops of these abutments below the top of the cut

3-7

Fig. 3-7. The Hardware Store, whose roof is in the lower part of the photo, has two chimneys that exhaust next to the wall of the Liquor Store. Their smoke has left black soot stains. I re-created them by drybrushing black chalk onto the beige wall of the taller structure.

to allow the street surface to match the top of the cut. Glue a piece of square wood painted Floquil Roof Brown on top of the foamcore as a footing for the bridge.

Now that the foundation of the city module is complete, let's add streets, buildings, and details.

Selecting Structures

I selected the structures for my city module with these specific factors in mind. Visitors had be able to see over the module to watch operation in the cut and yard entrance. Therefore, the structures could not be more than four stories high. However, since most buildings next to urban main lines are low-rise structures—tenements, industries, warehouses, etc.—this was prototypical.

I selected five building kits that met these criteria and named them to match local Boston establishments: The Triangle Drug Store, currently manufactured by SS Ltd., is a triangular building and a good fit for the narrow end of the module.

Design Preservation Models (DPM) Roberts Dry Goods building has a small footprint and fits next to the Drug Store as a Hardware Store. Jimmy's Barber Shop, marketed by Model Power, is a rectangular building that fits well next to the DPM structure as a Liquor Store. Superior Bakery, marketed by Con-Cor, fills the space between the Liquor Store and the side street. Finally, DPM's B. Moore Catalog Store, modified to a triangular shape, sits across the side street from the Bakery.

When placed side by side with the fronts on the curving main street, these structures fill the module, despite its odd shape.

Assembling and Detailing Structures

Prior to assembling most buildings, I usually spray-paint the walls, roofs, windows, and details (when these are separate castings) with Floquil so that each structure is a different color brick. Overwashes of Polly Scale Concrete, diluted with

Fig. 3-8. I made the billboard on the roof of the Bakery from a copier blowup of the front of a 1948 New Haven Railroad timetable. I tinted the logo, engines, and background by hand with watercolors.

alcohol, then work well for mortar. (We will look at these washes in greater detail in Chapter 6.) For my buildings, colors of brick and sash were chosen to represent Boston's architecture: Oxide Red with Hunter Green, Tuscan Red with Olive, Earth with Roof Brown, and Boxcar Red with Grimy Black and Dark Green work well. Weathering and detailing also contribute to the character of a structure, see fig. 3-7.

Since I wanted the Bakery building to look old, I put several mortar washes over it and drybrushed some vertical streaks on the walls using a light yellow chalk. I used dry-transfer lettering over the brick trim in the front to name the bakery, and added "Quality" and "Since 1905" in the brick arches above each of the two front windows. The bakery kit came with a roof-top billboard that I adapted to fit an old New Haven Timetable from 1948 showing three locomotives and the slogan "When You've Got to Get There Take the Train" on its front. I enlarged this drawing using a copy machine until

the locomotives and slogan fit within the frame of the billboard. I then hand-tinted the colors of the engines, the New Haven logo, and the background using watercolors (see fig. 3-8).

Other details, like window shades made from green and tan construction paper cut to different lengths, give structures a lived-in look. Since structures often have many windows where viewers can see right through the building, you may also want to add floors and a few walls cut from sheet styrene to break up the "hollow" appearance. Buildings should also receive roof details such as cyclone vents, chimneys, and skylights. Roof surfaces will have a tarred appearance if you paint them Grimy Black and paint the details Weathered Black with a wash of Rustall over the metal parts.

When all the structures are in place, viewers in the aisle behind the module can look over the buildings down into the yard (see fig. 3-9), while viewers in the operator area between the yard and main layout

can look at a complete South Boston street scene (see fig. 3-19).

Adding Sidewalks and Streets and Installing the Structures

It's no accident how my module fills a specific space, yet has enough room for streets and sidewalks. An easy way to ensure that you have the right amount of space is to make colored paper templates of the base of your buildings. Then move them around the top of the module until you get the effect you want (see fig. 3-10). After taping the templates to the module's top surface, lay thin, white tracing paper over the module so that you can easily see the dark top and the colored templates. Then draw sidewalks on the paper along-side the streets (see fig. 3-11). Depending on the location of a city module on your layout, you can place buildings and sidewalks on the module itself, or you can make a duplicate of its top from black posterboard and work on a bench.

For my module, I tried to keep the front street 3" wide with a 7/8" sidewalk on each side. The width of the street is often dictated by available space, so your streets may be narrower or wider than mine. I also extended the sidewalk under each structure, so there were no unrealistic gaps between building and sidewalk. At the end of the module, I curved the sidewalk around the edge of the catalog store to give the appearance of the front street turning a corner and running off the edge of the module. Since a city module is a *slice* of city, streets and sidewalks that run off the edge present no more problem than ending a hill at the edge of your layout.

When all of your sidewalks are designed, transfer their outlines to a piece of gray posterboard. Cut out each sidewalk, test-fit it on the module, and place the buildings on the sidewalk to check alignment. Then lightly mark the final outline

Fig. 3-9. This is what a visitor behind the city module sees when looking over the roofs of its buildings. The curve approaching South Station is in the foreground, while the throat of the terminal and adjacent yard are in the distance. Visitors feel as if they are standing in the middle of Boston.

Fig. 3-10. Here is how to position buildings on the city module's surface—the black triangular shape running from top to bottom in the picture. Trace the base of each building onto colored construction paper, which serves as a template. After selecting the location of each building, tape its template to the module's surface. If the module is at chest height, like mine, make a copy of its surface from black poster-board, and you'll be able to work at your bench.

Fig. 3-11. After taping all of the building templates in place, lay white tracing paper over the module and draw in the sidewalks with a black marking pen. A main street will run along the front edge of my module (in front of my left hand), and a side street (under my right hand) will run to the back of the module.

Fig. 3-12. Here's the top of the module with all of the sidewalks glued in place. Drybrush black chalk to make the darker areas of the sidewalks next to the streets. It will pick out the expansion joints. Glue in the wood alignment posts for the buildings as well. Both side streets and main streets run off the edge of the module, which is a slice of the city.

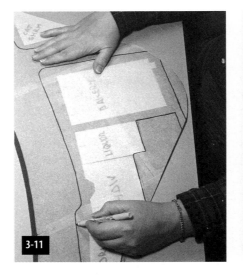

of each building on the sidewalk with a pencil and trim away any excess cardboard.

After spray-painting each sidewalk Floquil Concrete, scribe expansion joints into the surface (outside the building lines) with a hobby knife. Every city uses different spacing for these joints, but most fall in the 1-to-3-foot range. Start each scribe line at the street and run it up to the building outline. Lightly drybrush black chalk dust over the side-

walks, into the scribed lines to weather them, as shown in figs. 3-10 and 3-13. As a final step, glue each sidewalk in place on the top of the module's base so that you now have streets and a foundation for the buildings (see fig. 3-12).

Put each building in place and mark each corner with a pencil. After measuring the wall thickness, draw a second line to show each interior corner of the structure. Next, cut small pieces of ¼″ square wood and

glue them at each inside corner. These serve as alignment posts for each building. This makes it especially easy to remove a building for repair and put it back in its proper place (see fig. 3-12).

In order to complete the street running along the top of the cut, you should install a protective fence. Prototype mainline railroad cuts with streets running along them were common in cities like New York, Philadelphia, and Boston.

They dated back to the 1895-1920 period and had wrought-iron fences along their tops to prevent people from falling onto the tracks. (In more modern construction, pressed steel or tubular guardrails are used.) I selected Vollmer's no. 5133 fence, which has a stone base and posts with wrought iron in between. The fence comes in 4" sections, which when placed end to end follow the curve of the cut wall.

I painted the stonework Polly Scale Roof Brown and the ironwork Tarnished Black, and glued each piece of fence (using Walthers Goo) with its front against the wood edging that was previously installed on the street edge above the cut wall. Where the fence sections joined, I used styrene cement to hold them together. Figure 3-14 shows the completed fence.

City streets need white center lines, which you can add using 1/64" dry-transfer striping. Then draw street cracks and asphalt patches using a black Micron marking pen with a no. 02 point. Don't forget to add manhole covers, punched from aluminum foil with a paper punch, just off the street center line. Give each cover a coat of black wash of india ink (diluted 30:1) to make it look realistic, and mark four prybar holes with the point of the Micron no. 02 marking pen. Now we're ready for final detailing—back lots, vehicles, lampposts, pedestrians, and street signs.

Back Lots

The area behind city buildings can vary greatly. Industrial buildings have a paved area to serve loading docks. Residential buildings usually have weed-filled yards, which often become dumping grounds for junk and trash. Vegetation in these areas has a yellowish color, as the grass rarely receives water.

On my module (see fig. 3-15) the

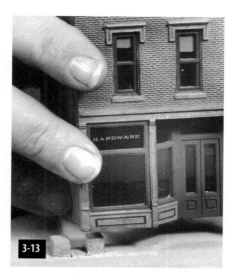

Fig. 3-13. Putting the Hardware Store in place. Note its alignment post, which fits just inside the front corner of the building. These posts allow structures to be removed and always fit back in the same place.

Fig. 3-14. This is a closeup of the wrought-iron fence on top of the front wall of the module. The fence is plastic sections, joined together and glued to a piece of stripwood running along the top of the cut wall. The vertical strip in the lower middle of the picture is where a vertical strip of stone paper hides the joint between two pieces of the paper.

Bakery and Hardware Store have rear loading docks that require paved access, while the Liquor and Drug stores have overgrown backyards. Since viewers can see the back of the module, these areas are as important to the module as the streets. To model a backyard similar to what you see in fig. 3-15 behind the Liquor Store, start by painting the lot with Polly Scale Earth acrylic paint. While the paint is still wet, sprinkle a mixture of Woodland Scenics earth and burnt grass fine foam onto the paint and allow it to dry. You can also add details like garbage cans, cases of empty cola bottle, and additional scenic texture, including small clumps of light green bushes and an area of straw-colored field grass. Install the field grass by cutting the bottoms of a number of strands level with a pair of scissors, then apply a small dab of Hobby-Tack adhesive to the bottom and hold them in place for 60 seconds. Cut the top of the grass to about 2 scale feet tall. Adding some burnt-grass coarse foam gives the yard a thoroughly unkempt look. Do this by gluing the foam in place by first spraying the yard with "wet water"—water with a few drops of liquid detergent added—using a cardboard baffle to keep the spray off the sidewalk and building sides. The detergent allows the cement to flow through the foam. Then, apply Woodland

Fig. 3-15. The backs of three of the module's buildings. From left to right: the edge of the Drugstore, a paved loading area behind the Hardware Store, the Liquor Store's fenced backyard, and the rear of the Bakery, which backs onto a sidewalk on a rear street. Cracks and patches help age the paved areas.

Fig. 3-16. This is a closeup of the backyard behind the Liquor Store. Unmowed tall grass and weeds, as well as the old tires, junk, and a rusting bicycle leaning against the opposite fence give the yard an unkempt and cluttered look.

Scenics Scenic Cement from an eye-dropper and allow it to spread through the foam.

You may want to surround the lot with a fence. I make fence boards from 2″ x 10″ HO scale stripwood cut 6 scale feet high. Start by gluing each board to two parallel 2″ x 4″

scale stringers placed 12″ from the top and bottom of the fence. Leave a small gap between each board—about 1/64″, just enough to see through. At every eighth board, add a fence post made from 4″ x 4″ scale stripwood. The two end posts extend 1/8″ below the bottom of the fence,

Fig. 3-17. Closeup of the wooden fence surrounding the backyard behind the Liquor Store. Each board has had a different number of ink washes, and broken boards simulate a very weathered fence. The ad is a dry transfer.

Fig. 3-18. Achieve additional realism by gluing street signs to lampposts.

while the middle posts are cut flush with its bottom. You can distress the outside of the fence by running a fine wire brush vertically over the boards, and even break off several boards where they join the top and bottom stringers, to leave an occasional gap in the fence. I also added some advertising signs from a set of dry transfers and cut through the signs along the gap between the boards. You might even want to brush on a dark wash (1 part india ink to 30 parts alcohol), to make some boards darker than others (see fig. 3-17). As a final step, drill a 3/32″-diameter hole for the posts of each piece of fence and secure the posts in place with gap-filling cyanoacrylate (CA).

Age the paved area behind the Hardware Store by drawing cracks and patches on the asphalt with a Micron no. 02 pen. Glue a few small pieces of green foliage along the foundation line of the structure to simulate weeds. Place trash cans, a barrel, and several crates around the loading door. Add an old pickup

3-19

3-20

Fig. 3-19. Looking down the side street between the Bakery (left) and Catalog Store (right), we can see the front street of the module and beyond that the yards (with a brand new New Haven PA-1 on a siding). Details along the sidewalk—a parcel postbox, a hydrant, pedestrians, and a lamppost at the intersection—as well as a 1948 Mercury sedan give life to the scene.

Fig. 3-20. Looking along the front street of the module past the Drugstore clearly reveals the slice-of-city effect. This concept allows you to build just a small piece of city yet capture the bustle of urban scenery in a minimal space.

truck with a workman unloading it and a clerk checking invoices to give the area some life.

Detailing the Street

It's the little city details that add interest to a scene. Since my city module depicts a prototype (Boston) during a specific time period (the late 1940s), I selected and painted the details accordingly (see fig. 3-18).

Plastic lampposts by Campbell Scale Models, painted Polly Scale Dark Green, closely match Boston's paint scheme (but black, gray, and tan are appropriate too). You can even add some road signs to the lamppost, such as "No Parking." As seen in fig. 3-19, glue the lampposts to the sidewalks, next to the curbs. You should add hydrants to the sidewalks and a fire alarm box, painted red, on a post at an intersection. A parcel box (free-standing, round-topped mailbox), and a letterbox fixed to a lamppost also add detail to a city scene. Be

aware that the U.S. Postal Service painted all of these boxes Pullman Green prior to the 1960s.

Finally, vehicles and people add life to your city module. Having been brought up in the middle of New York City, I know that streets can look very different depending on the time of day. On a weekday, early in the morning and late in the afternoon, streets have more cars and people than during the rest of the day. My city module portrays a midday scene rather than rush hour and includes only retail and residential structures, which determined my selection of vehicles and people. I placed seven automobiles and light delivery trucks on the streets for traffic. When modeling the late 1940s, remember that World War II had been over for only three years, and new vehicles were still somewhat scarce compared those from the late 1930s and very early '40s.

Like vehicles, the number of

pedestrians varies by time of day. At rush hour or lunch break sidewalks are crowded; during work hours, tradespeople are usually going somewhere, housewives are out talking with one another, children may be on the streets if it is a summer day. On my module I included 16 people dressed for late summer or early fall.

The city module is a very practical method of conveying an urban environment in a limited amount of space. Its shape is variable, so it can be designed to fit into virtually any layout. Because it is a slice taken out of a city, viewers can see the buildings and streets from all sides, which allows you to add normally unseen areas such as backyards or alleys. Finally, if properly joined to a cut, it can be used as a transition between rural and urban settings. This requires a minimum amount of physical space but conveys the illusion of the prototype railroad entering and running through a large city.

Building Street Bridges

Here is the first bridge, complete with vehicles and pedestrians. In this shot it is obvious that the bridge carries a busy street over an equally busy railroad in the middle of a city.

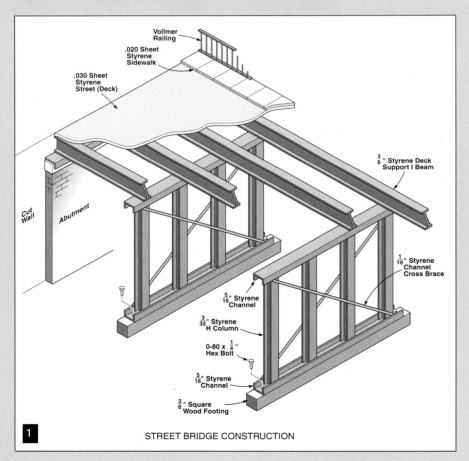

Vollmer Railing

.020 Sheet Styrene Sidewalk

.030 Sheet Styrene Street (Deck)

Cut Wall

Abutment

$\frac{3}{8}$ " Styrene Deck Support I Beam

$\frac{1}{16}$ " Styrene Channel Cross Brace

$\frac{5}{16}$ " Styrene Channel

$\frac{3}{32}$ " Styrene H Column

0-80 x $\frac{1}{4}$ " Hex Bolt

$\frac{5}{16}$ " Styrene Channel

$\frac{3}{8}$ " Square Wood Footing

1

STREET BRIDGE CONSTRUCTION

Fig. 1. This drawing shows the construction of the street bridges over the cut, which is typical for most street overpasses. Use styrene structural shapes and sheet to fabricate both bridges. To gain access to the track, remove the bridge by loosening the 0-80 x $\frac{1}{4}$" hex-head machine screws that hold the bottom of its piers to their wood footings.

To give the illusion that the cut on my layout runs through the city, I built two bridges over it for local streets. Street bridges are relatively simple structures made of structural steel with a deck carrying the pavement. To save cost, free spans were rarely longer than 50 feet; and support piers, also made from structural steel, were located between the tracks. Where long free spans were required, a truss bridge carried the street over the railroad.

Using Evergreen and Plastruct styrene structural shapes, I built my bridges in place running from the abutments on the outer wall of the cut to the freestanding anchors, where the inside of the cut would have been. The first bridge, where the tracks begin to fan out before the curve into the terminal, crossed nine tracks and called for two supporting piers. I built the second bridge, which entered the cut from the main layout, across six tracks with a single support pier in the middle. Using the first bridge as an example, here's how you can build one like mine.

First, cut a strip of paper, 3⅞" wide (the road width for both bridges) to the length of your bridges, to serve as a working template, and lay it across the tracks between abutments. Draw in the two support piers, making sure that they have clearance for the trains on adjacent tracks. Now cut a footing for each pier from ⅜" square wood, extending ¼" beyond the edges of the bridge, paint it Roof Brown or Aged Concrete, and glue it between the tracks across from the bridge abutment. Next, cut a piece of ⁵⁄₁₆" plastic channel (with the sides of the channel facing up) the same length as the footing, and drill a no. 56 hole through each end of the plastic into the wood. The holes are used for anchor screws (0-80 x ¼ hex-head machine screws) to hold the pier

Fig. 2. Assemble the piers for the first bridge over the cut and attach them to their footings with small screws (visible on the bottom of each pier to the left of its first column).

Fig. 3. Glue the I beams, which support the bridge's deck, on top of the piers. Do this piece of construction with the bridge in place.

Fig. 4. Glue the sheet styrene bridge deck onto the support beams. When dry, remove the screws from the piers and lift out the structure for painting and detailing.

in place. When removed, the entire bridge assembly can be lifted out to access the track beneath. Use an 0-80 tap to provide a thread in the wood footing—wood will hold the threads if the screws are installed and removed carefully. Then bolt the bottom channel onto the footing.

Construct each pier as shown in fig. 1. Cut four equally spaced, vertical $^3/_{32}$" H columns so that their tops are $^7/_{16}$" below the top of the wall of the cut. Glue them with liquid styrene cement inside the $^5/_{16}$" bottom channel. Make a cap from a second piece of $^5/_{16}$" channel (with the edges of the channel facing down) and glue it across the tops of all four columns. Glue $^1/_{16}$" channels diagonally across the four columns, one on each side of the pier, for bracing. Place pieces of $^5/_{16}$" channel with one flange removed, giving it an "L" cross section, on the wood top of each abutment. Do not glue them (see fig 2).

Then glue four parallel $^3/_8$" I beams to support the bridge deck to the top of the piers, above each H column, and to the plastic L on the tops of the abutments. Where two pieces of I beam are necessary for the span, the joint between them rests on one of the support piers (see fig. 3). Make the deck (street) from .030" styrene, using the paper template as a guide. Add the thickness of the cut wall and the top of the bridge anchor to the length of the deck so its ends are flush with the outside edges of the cut. Put a dab of Styrene cement (from a tube) in five

places along each girder, and set the deck in place. Allow this assembly to dry overnight (see fig. 4).

Remove the bridge by taking out the 0-80 screws holding the piers to the wood footings, and run liquid styrene cement between the I beams and the bottom of the deck for extra strength. Scribe sidewalks, made from .020" styrene sheet cut $^7/_{16}$" wide, every $^1/_4$". Spray-paint them Floquil Aged Concrete, and glue them to the outside of the deck. Then mask off the sidewalks and paint the bridge's steelwork with Weathered Black to match the Boston prototype—green, gray, or tan would be correct for other cities. Finally, paint the street Grimy Black, as Boston bridges were paved with

asphalt. You can select other road surfaces for a bridge, depending on your preference. Many street bridges had concrete surfaces, while older bridges built around 1900 had brick or cobblestone surfaces, and in some cases wooden planks. If you want to have this type of surface, glue one of the available plastic brick or cobble street surfaces or individual wood planks onto the bridge girders instead of the .030" styrene sheet.

Add streetlights and Vollmer railings last. Note that older bridges usually had wrought-iron railings, while modern bridges from the early 1950s on had pressed-steel or tubular guard rails. I added vehicles and pedestrians to finish each bridge.

Fig. 5. The second bridge of the cut is shorter, as there are fewer tracks to span. Since it is farther away from the terminal, it gives the illusion of being nearer to the suburbs. A Boston type-5 streetcar rumbles across the bridge, while a passenger express accelerates outbound from South Station.

Through the 1970s, many cities had railroad freight lines running down streets in industrial and market districts. Modeling an urban railroad is unique, with in-street trackwork and sidings running into buildings. As in the prototype, freight trains compete with cars, trucks, and pedestrians on the city streets.

BUILDING A CITY
CHAPTER 4

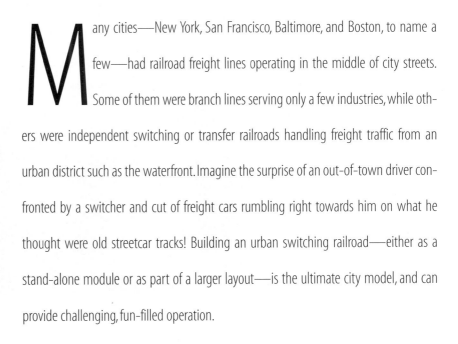

The Urban Railroad

Photo by Dave Frary

Many cities—New York, San Francisco, Baltimore, and Boston, to name a few—had railroad freight lines operating in the middle of city streets. Some of them were branch lines serving only a few industries, while others were independent switching or transfer railroads handling freight traffic from an urban district such as the waterfront. Imagine the surprise of an out-of-town driver confronted by a switcher and cut of freight cars rumbling right towards him on what he thought were old streetcar tracks! Building an urban switching railroad—either as a stand-alone module or as part of a larger layout—is the ultimate city model, and can provide challenging, fun-filled operation.

Fig. 4-1. In 1946 the Union Freight went 100 percent diesel and purchased five GE 44-ton switchers. While ideally suited to the tight curves and in-street operation of the line as shown in this 1946 photo, their 350 horsepower proved inadequate for trains longer than eight cars. They spent their short 7-year careers running MU'ed in tandem.

Fig. 4-2. After 1953 Union Freight leased Alco S-2s from New Haven for motive power. In the summer of 1966, cars and trucks dodge around no. 0600, working its way down Atlantic Avenue with one refrigerator car.

The Union Freight Railroad – My Prototype

Since I have lived in or near Boston, Massachusetts, for over 40 years, I chose to model the Union Freight Railroad. It was a subsidiary of the New Haven that ran down the middle of Boston's Atlantic Avenue and served the waterfront and commercial market district from 1872 to 1970. The Union Freight featured double-track, in-street operation with sharply curved sidings running into buildings and onto wharves. It connected Boston's two rail terminals—North Station (Boston & Maine Railroad) and South Station (New Haven and Boston & Albany Railroads). Cargo and fish from oceangoing ships were loaded onto freight cars and transferred by the UFRR to the yards at either terminal to be sent to destinations across the United States. Similarly, the Union Freight delivered produce from all over the country to Boston's wholesale market district. From 1901 to 1942, the UFRR ran underneath the Atlantic Avenue branch of the Boston Elevated so that freight trains, trucks, cars and pedestrians wove in and out between the columns of the "el."

Initially, the Union Freight operated 0-4-0 steam tank engines, covered with a boxcab to avoid scaring horses hauling wagons. These were replaced by three-truck boxcab Climaxes in the 1920s, which in turn

4-1

4-2

gave way to GE 44-tonners in 1946. The new diesels wore the same orange and green livery as the parent New Haven, but were lettered "Union Freight." Train speed was limited to 5 mph on the busy streets (see fig. 4-1). As the size of freight cars and the weight of trains grew, the 44-toners (even running in pairs) proved too light for the job. So in 1953 all of the GE engines were sold in favor of leased Alco S-2s from the parent New Haven (see fig. 4-2). The S-2s lasted until abandonment in 1970.

I decided to model the Union Freight as it appeared in the late

1940s, after the "el" was gone, and while the GE 44-tonners were in service. With only a change in motive power and rolling stock, my module can be updated to the 1950s and '60s, because Boston's waterfront was not modernized until the mid-1970s.

Design Considerations for the Union Freight Switching Module

I designed my Urban Railroad as an L-shaped switching module in a corner of the basement, across an aisleway from my Boston terminal. In the plans for the module, it looks

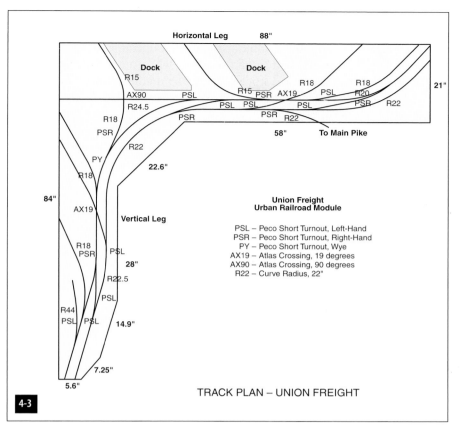

Horizontal Leg   88"

Dock

Dock

R15
R15   R18   R18
AX90   PSL   PSR   AX19   PSL   R20   21"
R24.5   PSL   PSL   PSL   PSR   R22
R18   PSR   PSR   R22
PSR
R22   58"   **To Main Pike**
22.6"
PY
R18
84"   AX19

Vertical Leg

R18
PSR   PSL
28"
R22.5
PSL
R44
PSL   PSL   14.9"
7.25"
5.6"

Union Freight
Urban Railroad Module

PSL – Peco Short Turnout, Left-Hand
PSR – Peco Short Turnout, Right-Hand
PY – Peco Short Turnout, Wye
AX19 – Atlas Crossing, 19 degrees
AX90 – Atlas Crossing, 90 degrees
R22 – Curve Radius, 22"

TRACK PLAN – UNION FREIGHT

4-3

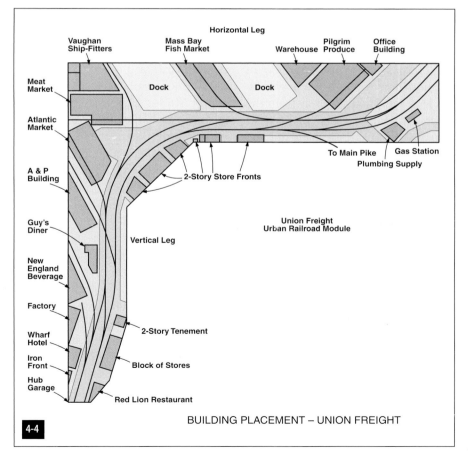

Horizontal Leg

Vaughan
Ship-Fitters   Mass Bay
Fish Market   Pilgrim   Office
Warehouse   Produce   Building

Meat
Market

Dock   Dock

Atlantic
Market

A & P
Building   **To Main Pike**   Gas Station
Plumbing Supply

2-Story Store Fronts

Guy's
Diner

Vertical Leg

New
England
Beverage

Union Freight
Urban Railroad Module

Factory

Wharf
Hotel   2-Story Tenement

Iron
Front   Block of Stores

Hub
Garage

Red Lion Restaurant

BUILDING PLACEMENT – UNION FREIGHT

4-4

4-5

Fig. 4-3. Printout of the track plan of the Urban Railroad Module generated by the CADrail 95 software. Label specific flextrack, crossing, and turnout components from the CADrail library to create a purchasing list.

Fig. 4-4. Add streets and buildings to the track plan. The CADrail software lets you create the final design on different levels (benchwork, track, streets, buildings), and you can print any individual level or a combination. This gives you the plans you need for each set of components of a layout.

Fig. 4-5. This photo shows the completed benchwork for the top leg of the Urban Railroad Module. The construction of the side leg (back of photo to the left) is similar.

like an L turned upside down. I have referred to the two parts of the module as the horizontal leg and the vertical leg, respectively. The module is connected to the Boston yard on my layout by a removable bridge. I can run freight cars from Boston across the bridge and then switch them on Atlantic Avenue. During switching operations, I remove the bridge so that operators and visitors can walk along the aisleway separating the Union Freight module from the main layout. The module's horizontal leg measures 21″ x 88″, and its vertical leg is 14″ x 84″.

Like its prototype, my module's design consists of a double-track line down Atlantic Avenue on the horizontal leg, curving through 90° and continuing onto Commercial Street on the vertical leg. (These are the two main streets on which the

Union Freight ran.) I included 11 sidings and three crossovers, requiring a total of 16 short, sharp turnouts, see fig. 4-3.

With all switches embedded in the street, I needed trackwork whose points would throw and lock without expensive switch machines. I chose Peco switches because they have sprung points that stay in the straight or curved position. By cutting a slot in the pavement over the throwbar, you can insert a pointed tool (for example, a bamboo skewer stick) into a hole in the throwbar, throw the switch, and the points will lock in position. I used Code 100 rail so the Peco switches would mate with Atlas crossings, required by the track design. Since only the very top of the rail shows above the street, the unprototypical height of C-100 rail is not visible.

I used Atlas Code 83 flextrack for the few sidings laid on private right-of-way (not in-street) and mated it to the C-100 switches with transition rail joiners. Finally, I designed structures that could be built from kits or building modules which captured the look and feel of the Boston prototype.

To speed construction, I converted my sketches into a final scaled plan using a computer CAD package (CADrail 95) on my PC. This software includes libraries for the Peco and Atlas track components, and can be drawn with different levels for benchwork, track, streets, and buildings. By printing each level separately, it's not hard to create easy-to-use construction plans like those shown in figs. 4-3 and 4-4.

Construction

I chose to support my switching module on traditional L-girder benchwork, consisting of girders made by gluing pieces of 1″ x 4″ and 1″ x 3″ pine together to form an upside-down L. Each girder rests on 2″ x 4″ legs strengthened by 1″ x 3″ bracing. The surface of the module consists of ½″ Homasote on top of ½″ plywood. You can use other materials such as Styrofoam or insulation board as a surface for your benchwork, but remember that it must support track, streets, and buildings, so the surface must be flat and level. I made harbor docks between waterfront wharves by cutting the shape of the dock out of the plywood/Homasote surface and gluing a separate piece of plywood across its bottom as a foundation for future water in the dock. Figure 4-5 shows the completed benchwork for the horizontal leg of the module; two docks are visible on its right side.

Lay the track directly on the Homasote using ⅜″ Micro Engineering spikes. Drive them through no. 61 holes drilled through the plastic ties in the Peco flextrack and turnouts. When laying in-street trackwork, be sure to paint a strip of Polly Scale Flat Black about ¼″ wide under each rail (see fig. 4-6), so that the Homasote or insulation board will not show through the ties when you look into the flangeway from the street. In addition, you might want to paint the inside of each rail the same color as the pavement so the shiny nickel silver will not show in the flangeway.

After laying all the track (see fig. 4-7) and the checking the gauge with an NMRA standards tool, it is time to make the module operational. Since the rest of my pike is wired using cab control and blocks, I used the same system on the Union Freight module for compatibility; however, there is nothing to prevent you from using DCC or any other control system of your own choosing. Due to the L shape of the module, and because its control area was also an aisleway, I needed two operating stations, one on each leg. I chose a memory throttle, made by Alpine Division Scale Models, which allows the UFRR operator to walk between stations while a train moves slowly along the module. I also built a control panel showing a schematic of the trackwork, and installed submini toggles to control power to portions of the trunk lines as well as to individual sidings. After completing all track and installing the throttle, I tested the module with a number of different freight cars and a couple of locomotives (see fig. 4-8).

Installing Streets

Over the years, I have used a variety of different materials for grade crossings and streets—plaster, wood, cardboard, and styrene, to name a few. While these materials are fine for short stretches of track in pavement, when faced with an entire layout of in-street track, you'll need materials that are easy to cut and fit around complex trackwork, as well as being removable—just in case.

For the pavement along the outside of each track, you can use posterboard, a type of cardboard .020″ thick available from most art supply stores. This material can be cut with a hobby knife and glued with a variety of cements. It holds paint well and has a good texture for HO pavement. First, draw the street pattern from the CAD rail plan onto the Homasote with a marking pen. Next, place pieces of tracing paper over the street and trackwork. Working with sections no larger than 8″ x 10″ (a size easy to handle), mark the location of the trackwork by sliding a lead pencil over the outer edge of each rail, including switches and crossings, leaving a line where the pavement will abut the track. Also mark the edges of the street. Transfer this pattern onto the posterboard using carbon paper. After cutting out the pieces of street with a hobby knife and metal

Fig. 4-6. Paint black lines ¼" wide under the rail and inner tie line of the in-street trackwork. This prevents the gray Homasote from showing between the ties when a viewer looks into the flangeways.

Fig. 4-7. Complete the trackwork on the top leg of the module. Note the two docks in the upper right of the picture. These will eventually contain water and barges.

Fig. 4-8. Install the control system and test the track with locomotives and freight cars. The secret of well-running urban in-street trackwork is to have everything running flawlessly before installing any pavement.

straightedge, trim each piece for a snug fit against the rails. On curves, use Baumgarten Ribbonrail track gauges as cutting guides to insure a smooth curve. Because posterboard tends to expand and contract with the moisture in a basement, make each street from several smaller pieces (6" to 10" long) to minimize buckling of the street's surface.

For the pavement in between the rails of the track, switches, and crossing, use .020" sheet styrene. Two factors dictate the choice of material. First, you'll have to carefully cut and trim the pavement between the rails to provide even flangeways. During installation only filing can obtain the correct fit and tolerances. Posterboard can not be filed; styrene can. Second, as the

backs of wheels rub against the inner pavement edges—particularly narrow sections at frogs and on tight curves—the edges of posterboard will fray during operation and eventually cause derailments. Styrene holds its shape without deforming. Make each piece of styrene pavement by marking the *inside edge* of the rails with a pencil on tracing paper; leave a ¹⁄₁₆" gap for each of the flangeways. Transfer this pattern to the styrene using carbon paper, and cut out the piece of pavement using a sharp hobby knife.

If all turnouts on your module are the same size, as mine were, you can mass-produce the inside pieces of pavement for the switches. Fabricate a set of three master templates for the center section (between the points)

and for each of the diverging routes from .040" styrene. By flipping the templates over, they fit both left- and right-hand turnouts. Holding each template on a sheet of .020 styrene, scribe its outline and then cut out each new duplicate. Complete the production cycle by clamping the duplicate parts, seven at a time, to the master template and carefully filing them until all parts are uniform.

In order for the Peco switch points to throw properly and insure trouble-free operation, there must be gaps between the inside piece of pavement and the switch points, somewhat larger than the gaps in the prototype. Painting the inside of the switch points the same color as the street surface makes the gaps look smaller. But leave the area where the

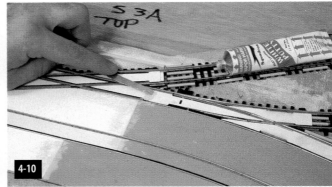

Fig. 4-9. Glue stripwood pavement supports to the ties of the turnout and siding in the upper right of the photo. Glue posterboard (gray), and styrene (white) to the supports to create the street's paved surface (at left). The yellow pieces of styrene (top left) are master templates to cut the pieces of turnout pavement which will be installed on switches (bottom center).

Fig. 4-10. Use plastic filler to fill any gaps between the styrene pavement and cast plastic guard rails of this crossing. When it's dry, sand the putty to form a seamless road surface.

Fig. 4-11. The Atlantic Avenue surface has been painted with Aged Concrete. The asphalt parking lot on the upper right is painted Grimy Black.

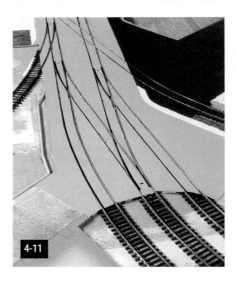

point touches the stock rail bare to insure electrical contact.

Make the pavement level with the rails by supporting it on stripwood. If the pavement abuts the outside of the rails or is between them, you can glue the stripwood to the ties with Walthers Goo; otherwise, glue it to the Homasote at the edge of the street (see fig. 4-9). The different sizes of stripwood you'll need are listed in the table on the next page. Note that the wood sizes shown should leave the street surface about 1/64" below the top of the rails. You'll be able to clean the rails (carefully) with a track-cleaning block without scratching the surface of the street. Cut the block so that its length is 1/16" to 1/8" wider than the track gauge. That way there is less tendency to scratch high points in the street pavement.

Once all of the posterboard streets are in place, fill the cracks between each piece with ready-to-use spackling compound (available at most hardware stores), using a small knifeblade to push it into the cracks and smooth the edges. Between the

rails, where the pavement is made from sheet styrene, use plastic model putty to fill any gaps (see fig. 4-10). Use putty between the styrene pavement and the plastic turnout guard rails, as well.

After the filler has set, sand it with fine sandpaper (no. 150), and then give the surface a final smoothing over with flexible emery cloth (no. 300). As you finish each section of street, test it with a locomotive and some freight cars, to insure clearance through the flangeways and smooth operation.

For the cobbled streets, glue an embossed, precolored Cobblestone Paper (Faller no. 601) on top of the posterboard/styrene street with Goo. To compensate for the added thickness of the cobble paper, make the stripwood supporting the street 1/64" lower in cobbled areas. See the table on the next page.

Painting and Finishing the Streets

Throughout the 1950s most urban railroads, including the Union Freight, operated on track embedded

in concrete or cobblestone streets. Many of these streets were resurfaced with asphalt in the 1960s. In 1948, the period that I model, most of Atlantic Avenue was paved with concrete, although there were still stretches of cobblestone. Two kinds of concrete were used: a yellowish mix for the main street and a darker mix with coarser aggregate next to and between the rails. The street surface was in very poor shape, with many potholes caused by harsh New England winters. They were filled with tar, as were the cracks and expansion joints between the sections of concrete. The concrete between the rails was further darkened by grease dripping from locomotives. In addition, when the Atlantic Avenue Elevated was torn down in 1942, the holes left from its support columns were filled with concrete, much grayer than the rest of the street. Intersecting side streets were

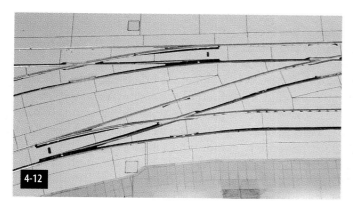

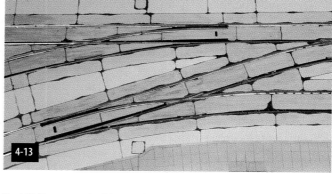

Fig. 4-12. Draw expansion joints on the Atlantic Avenue concrete pavement with a Micron pen. Note the square patches in the center of the picture where the "el" columns once stood.

Fig. 4-13. Tint the concrete sections next to and between the rails with an ink wash. Add tar patches with a Micron pen where chunks of concrete have been dislodged next to expansion joints. Glue the sidewalk in place (bottom of the photo).

Fig. 4-14. Complete Atlantic Avenue's pavement by airbrushing the pavement between the rails and along the traffic travel lanes with Engine Black to simulate oil drippings. Compare this picture to fig. 4-1, which shows the "real" Atlantic Avenue.

paved either with asphalt or cobblestone. In fig. 4-1, taken in 1946, you can see the poor condition of the pavement, which lasted until the freight line was abandoned and the tracks were removed in the 1970s. To replicate the look of this prototype, follow the five-step process below:

• Paint the street surface with two coats of Polly Scale Aged Concrete (see fig. 4-11).

• Outline expansion joints in the street surface with a Micron high-quality black marking pen (available in art supply shops) with a no. 02 fine tip. I added the concrete patches where the "el" columns had been by making a square template 3 scale feet on a side and drawing squares on each side of the tracks with the pen. Paint the concrete inside this square with Polly Scale Concrete. A section of street with expansion joints is shown in fig. 4-12.

• Using a no. 3 brush, tint the concrete sections on each side of the tracks with a wash of india ink diluted 60:1 with alcohol. Then, tint the pavement between the rails a darker india ink wash of 30:1.

• Draw in asphalt pothole patches and gaps in the expansion joints with a Micron pen with a no. 05 tip.

STREET SURFACES AND SUPPORTS

Street Surfaces

STREET SURFACES

Material:	Concrete	Asphalt	Cobblestone
	Posterboard or styrene (on switches)	Posterboard or styrene (on switches)	Faller no. 601 paper on posterboard or styrene
Color:	Aged Concrete	Grimy Black	Precolored, embossed

SUPPORT STRIPWOOD SIZES (C-100 prefab track)

	Posterboard and styrene	Cobble
On Homasote:	HO 12″ x 12″ (scale)	HO 10″ x 10″ (scale)
On outside ties:	¹⁄₁₆″ x ³⁄₃₂″	³⁄₆₄″ x ³⁄₃₂″

SUPPORT STRIPWOOD SIZES (C-83 prefab track)

	Posterboard and styrene	Cobble
On Homasote:	HO 10″ x 12″ (scale)	HO 8″ x 10″ (scale)
On outside ties:	³⁄₆₄″ x ³⁄₃₂″	HO 3″ x 8″ (scale)

There should be many such patches covering holes caused by the vibration of passing trains next to the rails, and between the concrete sections abutting the tracks. Figure 4-13 shows the results of steps 3 and 4.

• With an airbrush and Engine Black paint (either Polly Scale or Floquil) add the grease stains between the rails of the tracks and along the traffic lanes of each street. After the paint is dry, remove it from the top of the rails using a track cleaning block.

Paint asphalt road surfaces using two coats of Polly Scale Grimy Black and draw in cracks with a Micron pen. Darken the travel lanes on all streets with an airbrush, as described above. Where the "el" columns had been removed from cobblestones, run a sharp hobby knife with a no. 11 blade around the edge of the column template and carefully remove the top (colored) layer of the cobblestone paper from inside. Put a fine coat of white glue inside the column hole to smooth the surface of the paper; when it's dry, paint it with Polly Scale Concrete. (The condition of your city's streets may not be as bad as Atlantic Avenue, but these techniques will make their pavement look realistic.)

Building Foundations

When you build an urban railroad, the base of your buildings must be at the same level as the surface of the street (i.e., at the top of the rails). Therefore, you'll have to construct a foundation underneath your buildings, the same height above the top surface of benchwork as the street. To match my C-100 track, I found that pieces of ⅛"-thick foamcore with posterboard on top was the same height as the streets. So I cut pieces of foamcore into 1" x 2" rectangles and glued them to the Homasote about 1" apart to support the posterboard (see fig. 4-15).

You can cut the deck under each building from the same posterboard used for the streets. To compensate for the expansion and contraction of the Homasote or any other benchwork surface you may use, build up these large areas from smaller sections (see fig. 4-16). This provides expansion joints. I glued my posterboard surface to the foamcore supports with Goo, which gives a slightly flexible bond. Fill the cracks between sections with lightweight spackling compound to form a smooth, continuous surface. Paint the surface with Polly Scale colors to match the pavement around each building.

In several places on the module, there were no buildings or pavement—yard tracks, vacant lots, places where the street ran next to the edge, and so on. Here, the Homasote became the ground. I used Sculptamold to provide a slope from the pavement to the ground (see fig. 4-17). Paint all these ground areas with earth-colored latex paint. While the paint is wet, sprinkle Woodland Scenics foam onto it, just as you did in the backyards in Chapter 3. When the paint dries, cementing the foam in place, blend road dirt into the foam with a wash of Grimy Black (see fig. 4-18). We will look at completing the vacant lots later in this chapter.

Installing Sidewalks

Atlantic Avenue had sidewalks along those blocks that contained stores and offices. If a structure required rail or truck access, the pavement ran to the building line. You can make sidewalks from posterboard, as I did in Chapter 3, or from sheet styrene. For the Union Freight module, I chose .030" styrene, since you can make deeper, more visible expansion joints with styrene than with posterboard.

Divide the top surface of the styrene into 3' square paving blocks and use a scriber and straightedge to mark the joints between blocks. Where the sidewalk meets the street, scribe curbstones 6" wide by 6' long. Airbrush the sidewalk with Floquil Concrete. When it is dry, gave it a wash of india ink diluted with 60 parts of alcohol. This settles into the grooves between the paving blocks so they are quite visible. Finally, paint the curbstones with two different shades of Polly Scale gray. (I used Milwaukee Gray and CP Gray to match the shades of granite used for Boston curbstones.) Then glue the sidewalk in place, overlapping the completed street edge by at least ¹⁄₁₆".

To further detail the streets, add etched brass manholes and storm drain covers made by Model Memories. First paint the area under where each drain or manhole will go with Engine Black. Next give the drain cover a coat of Floquil Old Silver (Gunmetal is a good alternate) and add a wash of india ink diluted with 30 parts of alcohol. Glue each fixture in place with cyanoacrylate cement. Figure 4-19 shows a completed sidewalk next to a cobblestone street with a storm drain.

Constructing the Buildings

The design of the Union Freight module calls for three categories of urban buildings:

• Low, two- to three-story residential and commercial structures running along the inner edge of the module between the operator area and Atlantic Avenue. Viewers have to look *over* these buildings and *into* the street with its switching railroad, which adds realism. The structures also must be low enough so the operator can reach across them to throw switches, uncouple cars, and re-rail trains if necessary. These buildings are divided into blocks with side streets between them. The side streets are in front of turnouts for easy access by the operator.

4-15

4-16

4-17

Fig. 4-15. Install ⅛" foamcore blocks between the siding and dock to support buildings and parking lots. Later, you'll glue sections of posterboard to these blocks to form pavement and the building foundations

Fig. 4-16. Glue the posterboard over the foamcore. Fill the seams between individual sections with lightweight spackle and lightly sand them smooth.

Fig. 4-17. Spread Sculptamold on top of the Homasote where there is no pavement to form vacant lots. You'll add scenic foam in a later step.

Fig. 4-18. Close-up of the transition from in-street track to private right-of-way. Use Sculptamold to create the "slope" from the pavement to the ground. Add scenic foam, giving the foam between the rails a black ink wash to simulate oil stains.

4-18

• Large multistory structures—markets, warehouses and freight terminals—between Atlantic Avenue and the wall of the basement. Since sidings curve off turnouts in the avenue and run at an angle either into these buildings or parallel to their loading docks, the structures are at an angle to the street. So each building is a unique shape and must be custom-built.

• Building flats and backdrops glued to the wall behind the module. Use commercially available flats—about 90 percent full size—immediately behind the three-dimensional, multistory structures, and place photo backdrops of real buildings—30 to 50 percent full size—behind the flats. This adds forced perspective and depth to the module.

Build the structures in the first category from stock DPM, Walthers, and City Classics kits. Select the structures to give the look and feel of Atlantic Avenue in the late 1940s; you don't have to try to duplicate specific buildings exactly. To differentiate the structures, paint them various shades of brick and add different colors of storefront trim that which matches Boston's (and other cities') architecture from the late 1940s. Specific color suggestions can be found in Chapter 5. I built most kits "as is"; but where the tracks and avenue went around the 90° curve between the legs of the module, I cut the sides and ends of the structures to fit the street (see fig. 4-20).

Each building in the second category has a unique shape dictated by the trackwork. On my layout, I built only one of these structures unchanged from a stock kit; I used Walthers Roberts Printing Co. for it. I painted the cast concrete skeleton Floquil Aged Concrete, and the brick curtain walls Boxcar Red. A straight siding, tangent to the curve of the avenue, ran into this structure.

For the remaining buildings, I used Walthers' Hardwood Furniture Factory, an all-concrete structure with architectural detail cast into its surface. However, I cut it down to three stories and kitbashed it into a triangular shape to accept a siding angling off the avenue. Construct the rest of the buildings from DPM or City Classics Building Modules. Make each structure look unique, even though it uses parts similar to those of adjacent buildings, by differentiating height, style of window, and color so that no two structures look exactly alike.

Where each structure meets the wall of the basement, simply having the roof end at the wall gives the building an unfinished look. Fix this problem by cutting top parapets from the discarded wall sections, and gluing them onto the roof where it meets the basement wall.

To make sure that each custom building exactly fit the space dictated by the sidings, first draw the outline of the building on a piece of tracing paper (see fig. 4-21), and then construct each wall from leftover kit parts or building modules.

When each wall is complete, test-fit it on the paper outline (see fig. 4-22). Then spray the completed wall sections for each structure with an appropriate brick color using Floquil paints. Select contrasting colors for adjacent structures. At the same time, spray the window sashes a color to complement the brick. A complete set of recommended colors for brick, architectural detail, and window sashes can be found in Chapter 5. After the walls are dry, give the

4-19

red/brown brick buildings a coat of Concrete Mortar Wash no. 1, while the beige structures receive a coat of Black Mortar Wash no. 1. (Exact formulas for these washes can be found in Chapter 5.) The wash picks out the mortar lines and details of the brick. On some of the red/brown brick structures, give the pilasters between modules and the line of vertically oriented bricks along the top of each module two coats of Concrete Mortar Wash no. 2. It will make these details stand out and further differentiate the building from its neighbors.

At this point, add large signs to some of the walls to identify the owner or advertise products. Next, glue the window sashes in place—making sure to scrape the paint off the flange holding the window to the back of the wall so the glue will stick to it. Finally, cement Main Street Graphics windows (with shades or blinds printed on them) to the back of the window sash with Goo.

To hold the completed wall sections at the proper angle to fit the outline, copy the angle between the sides onto a piece of .040″ styrene using carbon paper. This makes a triangular gusset plate to hold the sides together. You need to have one gusset plate between each story of the building, as well as one under the roof line and one at the base of the building. Cement the gussets to the back of the plastic walls, and sand the

Fig. 4-19. Install styrene sidewalk at the edge of cobblestone streets. Use a black ink wash to bring out the scribed expansion joints and paint the curbstones different shades of gray. The storm drain is etched brass; paint it with Floquil Old Silver, and glue it over a section of the cobbles painted flat black.

edge of the wall to align with the angle of the gusset using the outline as a guide. Then make floors out of .020″ styrene, one for each story, so viewers cannot look through the structure and see out the back windows of the floors above and below. Paint the upper surface of each floor black or dark brown. Cement short sections of ¼″ styrene angle to the inside of the wall between each story to support the floors. If a building intersects the wall of the basement, cut a piece of .020″ sheet styrene to cover the rear opening. Figure 4-24 shows an exploded view of how these parts go together.

When all of the walls for each structure are assembled and painted, glue them together, one at a time, by applying plastic cement to the gussets and edges of abutting walls. Before adding the sheet styrene back to those buildings placed against the basement wall, glue styrene structural shapes (usually a ½″ square or I beam) across the open back of the building. Put one at the roof line and one at the base to strengthen the structure. Then insert the roof and floors into the building and cement

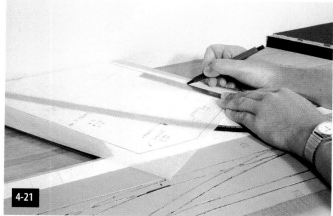

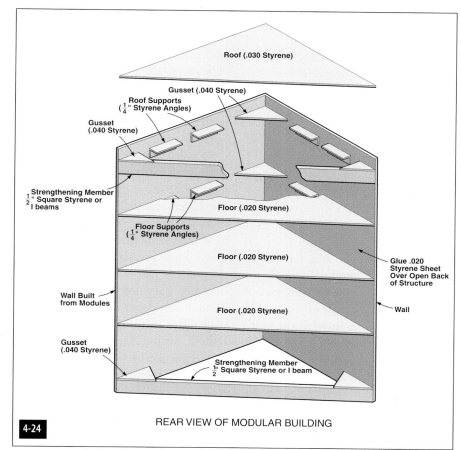

REAR VIEW OF MODULAR BUILDING

Roof (.030 Styrene)

Gusset (.040 Styrene)

Roof Supports
($\frac{1}{4}$" Styrene Angles)

Gusset
(.040 Styrene)

Strengthening Member
$\frac{1}{2}$" Square Styrene or
I beams

Floor (.020 Styrene)

Floor Supports
($\frac{1}{4}$" Styrene Angles)

Floor (.020 Styrene)

Glue .020
Styrene Sheet
Over Open Back
of Structure

Wall Built
from Modules

Floor (.020 Styrene)

Wall

Gusset
(.040 Styrene)

Strengthening Member
$\frac{1}{2}$" Square Styrene or I beam

Fig. 4-20. Where the two legs of the module meet, Atlantic Avenue goes around a 90° bend. Modify the shape of each of the low structures between the visitor area and the street to follow the curve.

Fig. 4-21. Draw the outline of a specially shaped structure on tracing paper. Since you'll kitbash the building from DPM modules, the length of the sides should match that of one or more modules wherever possible.

Fig. 4-22. After completing each modular wall of the building, hold it alongside its neighbors on the template to ensure that the structure will be the correct shape and dimensions.

Fig. 4-23. Lower the completed building into place. Wood alignment blocks, one of which can be seen under the side of the structure, ensure its location. Paint the floor inside the walls concrete; the pavement in front of it is asphalt.

Fig. 4-24. Inside view of a partial building showing the placement of gussets, floors and floor support angles, and bracing across the open back of the structure.

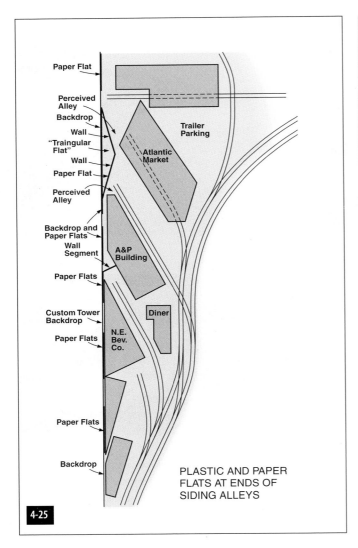

Fig. 4-25. Plan of the vertical leg of the Union Freight module, showing how paper and shallow plastic wall flats create a background for the three-dimensional buildings.

Fig. 4-26. Looking down a long alley between two buildings. Make the V-shaped flat at its end from scrap plastic walls; it makes the alley appear to curve out of sight to the right.

them to the support angles starting at the top of the building (roof) and working down to the bottom floor. Place the building in its final position. If it has a siding running into it or to an external loading platform, run a 50-foot automobile car into or alongside the structure to check clearances. Finally, add roof details and loading docks to the structure (see fig. 4-23).

To ensure that each structure will always sit in the same place, cement small blocks of ⅛″ square wood along the inside of each corner as alignment blocks (the same technique as I used in the Boston module described in Chapter 3). Then you'll be able to remove each building without disturbing its neighbors.

Flats and Backdrops

In Chapter 1, I discussed forced perspective, and in Chapter 2 I showed the placement of buildings, flats, and backdrops within the New Haven cityscape to achieve it. Unlike New Haven, the Union Freight module is very narrow, with no room to mount buildings and flats away from the wall. Therefore, you'll have to depend only on the relative sizes of the flats and backdrop to create forced perspective. In addition, since the module represents a particular city (Boston) at a specific time (late 1940s), you need a backdrop that includes the key landmarks of the Boston skyline. You can achieve both of these objectives in the steps described below. Figure 4-25 shows

were the different elements go on the vertical leg of the module.

• Ends of streets and alleys. Mount most of the structures on the UFRR module at an angle with respect to the basement wall. Looking down these alleys, a viewer can see from 1 to 4 inches of blank basement wall space. Hide the space at the ends of the narrow alleys with one or more building flats cut from a Walthers Instant Buildings sheet. Across the wide alleys, make a very shallow (less than ¾″) three-dimensional flat from two scrap pieces of brick wall. Glue these walls together in a very shallow V. The point of the V is in the middle of the alley, while its ends run behind the edges of the structures on each side (see fig. 4-25). This gives

Fig. 4-27. Pin paper flats and backdrop buildings of the Boston skyline to the wall of the basement behind the three-dimensional structures on Atlantic Avenue.

Fig. 4-28. The backdrop, flats, and three-dimensional buildings are now in their final location. Note how the different size of each element conveys a sense of distance through forced perspective, even though the entire scene is only 14 inches deep.

the impression that the wide alleys turn and run behind the main structures (see fig. 4-26).

• Flats. Behind the three-dimensional structures, place a line of Walthers city flats. The slightly smaller size of these printed buildings makes them appear to be a block or so behind the main structures. Where a flat is too short to be seen above the top of a three-dimensional structure, splice it to an identical flat from a second sheet to make it taller.

• The Boston backdrop. Immediately behind the flats, use computer-enhanced photographs of actual Boston buildings reduced 20 to 50 percent of full-size HO to create forced perspective for the module. In 1948, the downtown Boston skyline was dominated by a relatively small number of 10- to 15-story brick or concrete buildings, and one skyscraper—the 700-foot Customs House, which soared above everything else. This distinctive building, which still stands, is made of light beige granite, capped by a pointed roof. There is a large clock face on each side of the building just below the roof line. To capture this and

other distinctive examples of Boston architecture, a modeling colleague, Bill Vaughan (who is also a computer buff), used a computer-enhanced photographic process to make exact backdrop images of the Boston skyline that could be glued to the wall behind the flats.

To do this, obtain a good-quality 35mm color slide that shows the Boston skyline. The one I used was taken in 1960 from a wharf off Atlantic Avenue. Have the slide scanned and digitized at 1200 dots per inch (dpi) resolution onto a computer disk by a local camera shop. (This service costs between $5 and $25, depending on the resolution.) Then edit the digital images on a personal computer. (Note: most inkjet printers on the market now include at no additional charge photoediting software for both PC/Windows and Apple Macintosh computers.)

Create and print on an inkjet full-color images of the Boston buildings that are 20 to 50 percent of HO Scale—the smaller the size, the farther away the building looks (forced perspective). Using the cropping

commands of the software, make separate images of each structure or group of structures in the skyline, and print them out in two or three different sizes. Attach these images to the basement wall behind the buildings and flats on the vertical leg of the module with thumbtacks, and move them around (by trial and error) until you get the best perspective effect. Figure 4-27 shows the buildings, tacked to the wall, in their final locations.

Once the position of all backdrop elements is fixed, cut each out and lightly mark its location on the wall with a pencil. Fill in the holes left by the thumbtacks with spackle, sand each patch, and paint it the same light (sky) blue as the surrounding basement wall.

Print the final images on an inkjet printer, using "bright white" (regular thickness) paper. Since the buildings have been magnified many times from the original 35mm slide, the prints lose some resolution and appear slightly fuzzy. Far from being a detriment, however, this fuzziness creates the illusion of haze on a warm day, adding to the sense of distance.

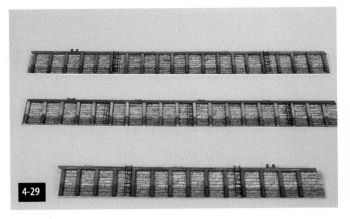

Fig. 4-29. Here are the completed wall segments of one of the docks before installation. The dark band along the lower side of each wall is the high-tide line.

Fig. 4-30. The dock is now complete. A produce barge is moored along the wharf to the left, and harbor water with waves can be seen on the right. The photographic backdrop shows the East Boston waterfront across the harbor and was generated on a computer from a slide taken in 1960.

• Putting it all together. Using Super 77 spray adhesive, attach each piece of backdrop to the wall in the following order:

1. The printed photo images of the Boston buildings.

2. The Walthers flats. (These overlap the edges of the building photos and appear to the viewer to be in front of the photos.)

3. The plastic flats at the ends of the alleys.

The ultimate result creates an impression of distance through forced perspective using the relative sizes of the skyline and flats, see fig. 4-28, even though there was no space between the layers.

Completing the Wharves

The top leg of the Union Freight module, which represents Boston's waterfront, includes three wharves with two docks between them. As with the Boston skyline, I was able to obtain two slides taken in 1960 from the end of Lewis Wharf (on Atlantic Avenue) looking across Boston

Harbor. The first of these shows the buildings of East Boston, a view dominated by a large Boston & Albany Railroad warehouse; the second shows the heavy cruiser USS *Boston* being guided into the Boston Navy Yard by tugs. Scan, digitize, edit, and position these photo backdrops, using the same techniques as for the Boston buildings. Ultimately, create two backdrops, one from each slide; and glue them to the wall across the open end of each dock.

Many Boston wharves were faced with granite blocks in front of which were driven wooden pilings with timbers running along the top. Mooring bollards and cleats were bolted to the timbers to secure ships and barges. Make the wharf walls from pieces of ¹⁄₁₆"-thick basswood cut 1¹⁄₄" high. Make each wall in sections to match the shape of the wharf. Cover the inside of each wall segment (facing the water) with Faller no. 604 embossed stone paper. Cut pilings from ¹⁄₈"-diameter dowel, 1¹⁄₄" high, stain them with a mix of 1 part Floquil Walnut to 1 part Driftwood. Then glue them to the stone paper at 8-foot intervals. Since Boston is an ocean port, add a high-tide line by applying a wash of 1 part india ink diluted in 30 parts of alcohol, ³⁄₁₆" up the stone paper and pilings (from the bottom). Then glue 12" x 12" scale wood timbers across the top of the pilings and wharf wall. Use

Crow River mooring cleats and bollards, and paint them with Floquil Weathered Black plus a coat of Rustall for weathering. Glue them to the top of the timber with cyanoacrylate (CA). Finally, glue ladders leading from the water to the top of the wharf at every sixth piling. Figure 4-29 shows three of the completed wall segments.

The next step is to paint the plywood floor of each dock with two coats of dark blue acrylic enamel. Add some black towards the middle of each dock to give the effect of greater depth. Glue the wharf walls in place.

Make the water for the docks in three steps. First cement a piece of clear styrene across the open end of each dock, with its top ¹⁄₄" above the surface of the dock. Second, pour a layer of clear Envirotex epoxy ¹⁄₈" deep and allow it to set for three days.

When dry, add any ships or barges you want on top of the Envirotex, holding them in place with a drop of Goo. I had two water-line barges custom-built for me by a Connecticut nautical artist and modeler, Steve Cryan. I moored one in each of the two docks. The first was a produce barge, used through the 1950s for transferring fruits and vegetables around the harbors or port cities. The second was a tool barge, found in most ports.

Third, mold waves using Polyterrain Water Gel (available from

Polyterrain Inc., 2105 W. 18th St., Fayetteville, AR 72701). Step-by-step instructions for making realistic saltwater and mooring ships and barges to wharves can be found in my article titled "Modeling a Saltwater Port," which appeared in the September 1997 issue of *Model Railroader*. You can get a copy of this article by contacting *Model Railroader* magazine, 21027 Crossroads Circle, Waukesha, WI 53187. Figure 4-30 shows a completed dock with the barge, water, backdrop, and wharf buildings installed.

Completing Vacant Lots and Alleys

Where the tracks run near the edge of the benchwork and there is no room for a structure, add vacant lots between the sidewalk and the edge of the module. Wall off some of the lots using sections of board fence along the sidewalk. I used plastic fence from Central Valley; it is strong and has excellent grain detail. Wood fences in the middle of a city receive a lot of wear, so break off the top or bottom of some boards in the fence casting and remove others altogether. Where a board is missing, file the fence stringers (behind the boards) to compensate for the missing board's thickness. Paint the fence with Floquil Earth. Leave a few boards the base color (these look like new replacements), and tint the rest with a wash of india ink diluted 30:1 with

alcohol. Give the boards one, two, or three coats of wash—the more coats, the older the board looks—in a random pattern to make each board unique. Note that you must tint the back of each board the same as the front. Using a set of Woodland Scenics dry-transfer ads, which includes some election posters for Dewey and Truman—perfect for my 1948 period—apply posters and ads to the front of the fence facing the sidewalk to add realism. Slice the ads at the joints between boards, and then tint the posters with a wash of 60:1 india ink to age them. For really old posters, use several coats of wash and scrape away pieces of the dry transfer altogether with the point of a modeler's knife (see fig. 4-31). Complete the vacant lots by adding weeds, old tires, and junk.

Between many of the buildings are alleys, most of which the viewer can look down, so they must be detailed. Some of these alleys are paved with concrete and need weeds growing through the expansion joints and cracks. To create this effect, paint Woodland Scenics Cement into the cracks using a fine no. 3/0 brush. Remember to rinse the brush in water after two or three strokes to keep its bristles from gluing together. Then sprinkle some fine weed and burnt grass foam onto the wet cement, and allow it to dry. After vacuuming away the excess foam, you have weed-filled cracks (see fig. 4-32).

Fig. 4-31. Here's a section of plastic board fence, weathered to look like aged wood, by applying an ink wash in a different number of coats to each board.

Fig. 4-32. Weeds poke through the expansion joints in the concrete sidewalk under the garbage cans in this backyard. To create them, brush a little scenic cement into the crack and sprinkle weed scenic foam onto it.

In all of the visible alleys, add some garbage cans and junk (from Builders-in-Scale), painted and weathered with india ink washes and Rustall. Painting suggestions for these details are given in Chapter 6. For those alleys next to markets and other industrial buildings, add old crates, barrels, and 55-gallon oil drums filled with junk and garbage. If the alley is wide enough, add an old car.

Detailing the Streets

Detailing the streets and sidewalks of the Union Freight Railroad module is basically the same as the city module described in Chapter 3, only there is much more of it. With many blocks to cover, I found that painting all of the details first and then installing them en masse was the most efficient way to proceed (albeit a bit tedious). Use one type of street light on Atlantic Avenue—the same plastic lampposts from Campbell as we used in Chapter 3 (these were similar to those used all over Boston, including parts of Atlantic Avenue); and a taller, wrought-iron hook-

4-33

4-34

Fig. 4-33. Looking down the completed Atlantic Avenue on the top leg of the module, we see a pair of Union Freight GE 44-toners moving a cut of reefers into the yard. The meat truck in the foreground waits as the train rumbles by. Along the right side of the Avenue are the docks and Mass Bay Fish Market, with the Boston skyline beyond them in the distance.

Fig. 4-34. A line of parked trucks and trailers at the Atlantic Market's loading dock. Such sights were common in downtown market districts through the 1970s.

Photo by Dave Frary

shaped lamppost from Woodland Scenics in the cobblestone section of Commercial Street on the vertical leg of the module. Paint both types of posts Polly Scale Dark Green to match Boston practices. Then install the lampposts on opposite corners of intersections and along each block at about 60-foot intervals. Paint fire hydrants Polly Scale Tarnished Black with Reefer Gray top and side domes and place them at the middle of every block and on the longer side streets. Paint fire alarm boxes Testors Flat Insignia Red, and install them every two blocks or every 150 feet, in areas where there are no intersections. Where there is a sidewalk (on the side of the street away from the railroad sidings), locate the alarm boxes on posts painted Polly Scale Tarnished Black. On the other side of the avenue and in the long alleys, mount the boxes on the sides of buildings, about 6 scale feet above the pavement. Then install letterboxes, painted Pullman Green—matching the olive drab colors of the U.S. Post Office in the 1940s. Attach them to lampposts at intersections, or on posts

of their own (painted Tarnished Black) in front of office buildings. I positioned freestanding parcel boxes (also painted Pullman Green) in the middle of blocks of stores along the avenue. A parcel box can be seen on the right sidewalk (next to the diesel) at the beginning of this chapter, and a fire alarm box is on the first column of the concrete building in the right center of fig. 4-33.

Cars, Trucks, and Trains

Unlike the City Module in Chapter 3, which depicted a typical city street, the Union Freight module represents a very busy waterfront and commercial market district. Therefore, during the daytime, the streets are filled with parked cars and trucks on the avenue. The vehicle loading docks of the industrial buildings and markets are lined with trailers either loading or moving into or out of place behind tractor trucks. Local delivery trucks are stopped along the sidewalks making deliveries or parked next to their owners' stores. And down the middle of the avenue run the Union Freight's GE 44-ton-

ners, hooting autos out of the way or leaving freight cars in the middle of the street to block traffic.

You'll need over 50 vehicles for the UFRR module, including a number of trailers being loaded, parked on their "landing gear." Since I modeled the late 1940s, I chose vehicles from that period. In Chapter 6, I have listed the manufacturers and availability of HO cars and trucks from the first half of the century (as well as those from more modern times). Most of the model vehicles for this period are cast resin, urethane, plaster, or metal kits, which must be painted and assembled.

Select about 35 cars and 15 trucks and trailers to populate the module, and paint them using photos and ads from the period. (I also called upon my own memories of growing up in the middle of New York City in the 1940s and visits to Boston in the early 1950s.) Color suggestions for vehicles of this period can be found in Chapter 6.

Place the vehicles on the module in realistic poses—parked, at building loading docks, or moving on the

Avenue or side streets. Don't glue the vehicles to the pavement, as you may want to rearrange them from time to time. Besides, picking them up makes them easier to dust. When placing the vehicles, check to make sure they are clear of the main line and all sidings, so they will not foul railroad equipment being switched. You can see many of the cars and delivery vans in fig. 4-33, and a line of trailers is at the loading dock of the Atlantic Cold Storage Warehouse in fig. 4-34.

Adding People

The Union Freight module is big, and you'll need over 200 people to populate it. About 60 percent of the figures are either workmen loading or unloading trucks and barges, or tradespeople and businessmen near the stores and office buildings. The remaining 40 percent are pedestrians—housewives, men not at work, and children. Most of the buildings on Atlantic Avenue were either industrial or commercial structures, and the residential premises over the shops were primarily rooms to rent rather than family dwellings—hence the low number of youngsters.

One of the things that I learned while populating my city was that simply going out and buying 200-plus, ready-to-install people is not necessarily the best course of action. From an economic standpoint—using Preiser as an example—an unpainted HO figure costs about 19 cents, while a factory-painted figure costs $1.75. Further, the colors that manufacturers paint their figures may not match the period you are modeling. Therefore, I chose to buy unpainted Preiser figures and decorate them myself with clothing colors appropriate to the late 1940s. I'll be discussing how to paint and, if necessary, modify figures in Chapter 6.

Operation on the Union Freight

While a detailed description of the operation of the Union Freight Railroad is beyond the scope of the book, a few words are in order. I made operating the railroad portion of the module as prototypical as possible to get the real feel of an urban switching railroad. One example is switching cars in and out of the sidings. In the prototype, the UFRR brakeman rode on the engine's front platform. When a car was switched into a siding, he jumped off with a prybar, lifted a metal plate in the street next to the switch, inserted the prybar in the hole, and threw the points. The engine then ran down the siding and dropped or picked up the cars with the brakeman operating the cut lever and attaching the air hoses. The engine then backed out, the brakeman reset the switch, replaced the cover, and hopped back on the locomotive for the next stop. On my module, there is a slot in the street over the throwbar. To throw a turnout, I use a bamboo teriyaki stick as a prybar, insert it through the pavement slot into a hole in the Peco throwbar, and set the switch. While a few of the sidings have Kadee uncoupler magnets, in most cases I insert the point of the same skewer between the coupler knuckles, rotate it, and the couplers part, dropping the cars either on a siding or in the middle of the street.

Throw the turnouts on the model Union Freight using the same manual technique as the prototype. Here, the prybar is a bamboo skewer; on the real UFRR it was a steel crowbar.

When a city building looks plain, there are a host of large and small details you can add to make it more realistic. A paint job that picks out architectural details, a clutter of vents and stacks on the roof, a wrought-iron fire escape on the outside wall, air conditioners in the windows, and advertising signs—painted on the wall or freestanding on the roof—are some of the techniques used to detail this building.

DETAILING A CITY
CHAPTER 5

Detailing
City
Structures

Photo by Dave Frary

When you build a model city, it is important to detail its buildings properly. This might include only those structures in the front row of a city backdrop, all of the buildings in a small, scenic city module, or the buildings nearest to the viewer in an urban railroad. Building details can be added using paint, three-dimensional fittings, roof hardware, weathering, signs, or any combination of the above.

Fig. 5-1. This three-story red brick commercial-residential building is typical of those found in most cities. Light gray granite lintels and sills on the windows enhance the brick facade, and a gray granite strip below the cornice defines the structure's roof line.

Fig. 5-2. Here's a brown brick office building that uses beige brick and stonework to enhance the corners and window lintels. Note the stone date plaque on the top corner of the building, the beige diamond-shaped stonework above the side windows, and the stone trim along the roofline. Many plastic structure kits have similar details, which can be enhanced by a good paint job.

Fig. 5-3. This tan brick office building uses brick indentations and panels to define the window lines and architectural lines of the structure. The windows, sills, and roof trim are dark brown, which complements the tan brick. Stone details include the building name plaque and ornamental trim at the top of the center line, which further enhance the building's facade.

Detailing Brick Buildings

Brick structures are probably the oldest buildings in your cityscape, dating back to late 1800s or early 1900s. The visible appearance of brick buildings was enhanced through the use of different sizes of brick, ornamental stonework to accent the shape of windows and doors (above and below the sash), cornice decoration near the rooflines, masonry name and date plaques, and keystones in arches. Figures 5-1, 5-2, and 5-3 depict brick structures, located in the center of a medium-sized city, that were built as long ago as the late 1800s and are still standing over 100 years later. They should last well into the new millennium.

Many urban building kits on the market today are quite similar to these prototypes. These kits have brick walls made of styrene, urethane, or Hydrocal with much of the architectural detail cast in. Let's look at some methods of enhancing these details.

Using Paint to Color Brick Walls and Outline Details

Virtually all model brick structures should be painted to look realistic, with the exception of those printed in color on paper or cardstock. While most manufacturers of styrene kits color the plastic, it rarely has the right shade or finish to depict the prototype accurately (see fig. 5-4). Most brick structures fall into three color categories: red brick, brown brick, and beige brick. The table on the right provides a list of railroad colors you can use to paint the brick walls of structures in each of these groups.

When coloring brick buildings, it is important to use paint that will dry absolutely flat. If the structure that you are painting has separate window castings, paint them separately, apart from the brick walls, using a sash color like those in the table. If the windows are cast integrally with the walls, paint them after the brick with a small brush. I spray-paint my brick structures with Floquil Railroad Paints (Polly Scale is an alternate if you prefer acrylics) using an appropriate base brick color for the structure.

I have found over the years that Floquil or Polly Scale gives the most realistic flat finish. Allow the base brick color to dry completely, at least 24 hours, before painting any details. Figure 5-5 shows two sides of a structure fabricated from a number of DPM modules and sprayed Floquil Tuscan Red—a good color for some red brick.

The next step is to paint any brick or stone detail work that may be cast into the walls of the building. At a minimum, this should include the sills below and lintels above the windows. Paint these details with a no. 0 or no. 1 brush, using a flat paint (Floquil or Polly Scale), making sure to cover the surface of the details while avoiding the surrounding bricks. If you have sprayed the base wall with Floquil, use Polly Scale for the details, as the acrylic will not attack the lacquer-based Floquil underneath or cause it to bleed through. Figure 5-6 shows the sides of the DPM modular structure with the arched brick above the windows and the sills below them painted with Polly Scale CP Gray.

Other details painted at this time include roof cornices and any other decorative stone or brickwork that may be cast into the walls. While the brick details of many industrial buildings were all the same color, urban offices and public buildings had architectural details such as plaques with date of construction or building name in a different, complementary color.

Adding Mortar

All three-dimensional (i.e., cast) brick structures have mortar lines between the individual bricks. Mortar can be added to the painted brickwork using two very different techniques: an overwash of diluted paint, or a mortar paste rubbed between the lines of bricks.

• Overwash. An overwash consists of a small amount of acrylic paint diluted with alcohol and water, with a little wetting agent (detergent) added. You brush the wash onto the painted brick wall after the base color has dried. The wetting agent helps the wash flow into the mortar grooves between the

Fig. 5-4. This view of the city module built by the Sheas (Chapter 2) shows seven brick buildings, each a different color. Although most people think of brick as being a brownish red, in reality it came in many different shades of beige, red, and brown; and the elements weathered it into many additional shades.

STRUCTURE COLORS
Brick Buildings
(Floquil and Polly Scale Colors are shown)

Base Brick	Brick/Stone Details	Window Sash
Red Brick		
Boxcar Red	Milwaukee Road Gray	Tarnished Black
Oxide Red	Concrete	Pullman Green
Southern Freightcar Red	Earth	Reefer Gray
Caboose	Aged Concrete	Hunter Green
Tuscan	Reefer Gray	Earth
Brown Brick		
Roof Brown	Concrete	Tarnished Black
Rail Brown	CP Gray	Pullman Green
Dirt	Milwaukee Road Gray	Hunter Green
Beige Brick		
Earth	Dirt	Roof Brown
Foundation	Roof Brown	Tarnished Black
Concrete	Dirt	Pullman Green
Aged Concrete	Reefer Gray	Pacemaker Gray

lines of brick, while the alcohol causes it to dry quickly and eliminates most of the wash from the surface of the bricks. The advantage of a wash is that it leaves a light coating on the surface of the brick, making it look worn and weathered,

and a heavier deposit in the mortar lines, defining them. For the best results, lay the wall on a horizontal surface while applying the wash and until it is dry.

I use two kinds of mortar washes: a Light Wash (no. 1 Wash), which

fills in the mortar grooves but leaves little color on the surface or the bricks, and a Heavy Wash (no. 2 Wash), which leaves a considerable amount of color on the brick, making it looked bleached. Use concrete-colored mortar wash for red or brown brick, and a black-colored mortar wash on beige brick. The formulas for mixing mortar washes are shown in the table on this page.

• Mortar paste. Mortar paste is available in several different colors by Scale Works Models. The paste is made from acrylic. You rub it into the mortar grooves with a moistened finger. Wipe the excess off the brick surface with a damp cloth. Depending on how skillful you are at removing it from the bricks, the result is quite uniform, and the mortar fills the grooves completely. Because most HO brickwork has rather wide mortar grooves, the final effect is to lighten the overall look of a structure, as the mortar is very prominent.

While the choice of mortar is up to you, Mortar Wash no. 1 on structures gives them a weathered look. Mortar Wash no. 2 helps give a heavily weathered brick surface; it also helps differentiate brick of the same base color. To get this effect, add mortar by applying a coat of Concrete Mortar Wash no. 1 to the entire DPM Modular structure as shown in fig. 5-7. To pick out the

brick detail over each window, carefully paint Black Mortar Wash no. 1 between the gray bricks over each of the windows. This makes them look darker and brings out brick detail.

The urban railroad module in Chapter 4 has five buildings constructed from DPM Modules. They are differentiated by window shape and brick color. To further differentiate one of the buildings, apply an additional coat of Concrete Mortar Wash no. 2 to the vertical pilasters between each modular segment as well as to the horizontal line of bricks along each module's top (see fig. 5-8). This lightens the pilasters and horizontal brick lines, giving the structure a unique appearance. To complete the walls, paint the window sashes Polly Scale CP Gray and install Main Street Graphics win-

dows with shades or venetian blinds printed on them.

Detailing Concrete Buildings

Two kinds of "concrete" structures are available as kits or modules:

• Concrete-skeleton buildings consist of reinforced concrete structural members, which are cast in place around either a steel beam or a group of steel reinforcing rods. The concrete forms a load-bearing skeleton on which the weight of the building rests. In older structures built from

Fig. 5-5. These two building sides were made from a number of DPM modules and spray-painted with base brick color using Floquil Tuscan Red

Fig. 5-6. The first step in detailing is to paint the arches over the windows and the horizontal line of bricks under the windows gray to show the brick architectural details.

FORMULAS
Mortar Washes

CONCRETE MORTAR WASHES (Use on red and brown brick)

Wash	Polly Scale Paint	Alcohol	Water	Detergent
no. 1 (Light)	1 part Concrete or Aged Concrete	9 parts	7 parts	2–3 drops
no. 2 (Heavy)	1 part Concrete	4 parts	3 parts	2–3 drops

BLACK MORTAR WASHES (Use on beige brick)

Wash	Polly Scale Paint	Alcohol	Water	Detergent
no. 1 (Light)	1 part india ink	60 parts	—	2–3 drops
no. 2 (Heavy)	1 part india ink	30 parts	—	2–3 drops

the late 1920s through the 1950s, the concrete skeleton is visible and forms a series of vertical and horizontal "concrete beams" with sections of brick—called a "curtain wall"—in between them. Walthers Roberts Printing Co. kit and City Classics Warehouse and Factory Modules are good examples of this kind of urban structure.

• Cast-concrete buildings are similar in concept in that they too have a load-bearing concrete skeleton; however, these structures are made entirely of concrete, including all outer walls. In many cases architectural decorative details are cast right into the walls. Also, there is no color distinction between structural members, the walls, or the details. Cast-concrete structures date from the 1920s, and in many cases large complexes of such buildings were built in a single industrial area. Bush Terminal, on the Brooklyn, New York, waterfront, consisted of dozens of identical concrete buildings covering many city blocks. The Walthers Hardwood Furniture Factory is a good model of a cast concrete building.

A good paint job is the only way to bring out the detail in concrete structures.

Using Paint to Define the Concrete Skeleton

To build a concrete-skeleton structure, use an airbrush and paint all of the walls in two stages. First, paint all parts of the visible concrete skeleton using either Floquil or Polly Scale paints. For a new structure, less than 15 years old, use Concrete; for older structures, Aged Concrete is more appropriate. Spray the entire wall, including the brick curtain, Concrete or Aged Concrete and allow the paint to dry overnight. Then mask off just the skeleton using chart tape—available in widths ranging from $1/64$" to $1/4$"

Fig. 5-7. What a difference a coat of light mortar wash can make in a building! This is the same wall that we saw in fig. 5-6.

Fig. 5-8. To further add distinction to the building in figs. 5-6 and 5-7, apply a heavy mortar wash to the pilasters and horizontal lines of brick. In addition, installing sash, window glass, shades, and venetian blinds gives the structure's walls a finished look.

at most graphic arts supply shops— leaving the brickwork uncovered. Then spray the brick either a red or brown using one of the colors in the table of brick paints. When this second coat has dried, see fig. 5-9, remove the masking tape and touch up any areas where the demarcation line between colors is not crisp. Next, add mortar to the brick using the Concrete Mortar Wash no. 1.

When all of the painting is complete, glue in the window sashes (painted separately from the walls) as well as either clear styrene or preprinted windows. Since most concrete-skeleton structures were used for industrial purposes, they had steel windows consisting of many small panes of glass. When one or more of these panes broke, it had to be replaced individually. During the 1930s and '40s, many companies replaced the broken glass with plywood or sheet metal welded over the sash opening. These solid pieces were painted either the same color as the sash, or a neutral gray. You can add realism to this kind of window by randomly painting over the clear window material on 5 to 20 percent of the panes (see fig. 5-10).

When all the walls of the structure

are complete, assemble the building, adding the roof and external details (to be discussed later in this chapter). At this point, darken the concrete skeleton a little, either by giving it a light coat of Black Mortar Wash no. 1 or by drybrushing black chalk dust onto the skeleton.

Using a Wash to Define Cast-Concrete Building Details

Painting a cast-concrete structure requires a somewhat different process. In this case, the building is entirely concrete and therefore only one color. The cast-in details of the prototype are enhanced by weathering, as dirt settles on the top (and sometimes the side) surfaces of the panels and other "sculptured" details. Spray the walls of cast-concrete buildings with either Floquil or Polly Scale Concrete or Aged Concrete. Then apply a coat of Black Mortar Wash no. 1 and allow it to run into the corners of recessed panels and into the seams between the walls and raised details. The dark wash will dry along these seams enhancing the detail and weathering the building (see fig. 5-11).

Fig. 5-9. Paint the walls of concrete-skeleton buildings in two easy steps. After painting the concrete skeleton, mask it off and paint the brick panels. When you remove the tape from the skeleton—as shown in this photo—a neat two-color wall emerges.

Fig. 5-10. When individual panes broke and were replaced with wood or steel panels in industrial windows, the window took on a checkerboard look. Model the same effect by simply painting a number of panes the same color as the steel sash.

Fig. 5-11. This is a typical all-concrete building. The architectural details are cast into the walls. You can highlight them by means of an ink wash, which will settle around the raised lines and panels.

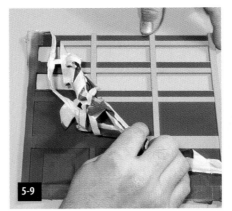

Detailing Modern Glass-Walled Buildings

As I noted in Chapter 1, the only high-rise, modern glass-wall structure kits are a few in N scale (1:160). Where such buildings have been constructed in HO and larger scales, the glass wall surface is made of Plexiglas, with styrene or cardboard strips for panels. You can make stainless metal trim and accent lines from chrome tape, available in hobby shops catering to car modelers.

Most modern (post-1950) buildings are made from precolored materials that do not easily weather. For example, "clear" or "tinted" windows may alternate with vertical or horizontal panels made of glass, painted or enameled steel, stainless steel, or some other decorative material. Common colors for the decorative "accent" panels include green, aqua, blue, aluminum, stainless steel, yellow, or even coral.

Modern structures are usually showcases for their owners (or even the cities in which they are located); when they get dirty they are washed—windows and walls. This is done by lowering a scaffold working platform from the roof on cables. Workers on the scaffold clean the building chemically or with steam. A cleaning crew consisting of a scaffold,

made from strip styrene with a couple of window washers at work is a nice detail to add to a modern structure. Leave that portion of the building that has been washed shiny, and spray a very light coat of Dullcote from an airbrush over the "dirty" portions to dull them down.

Adding External Details to Building Walls

Depending on the kind of building you are modeling, the number of external details on the walls can range from many to none. A general rule of thumb is: the older the building the more items have been added to its walls over time. Modern structures are self-contained—heating, air conditioning, fireproof stairwells, etc.,

are built in from the start. But older brick structures dating from the early 1900s had these details added externally over time. Let's look at a few of the more common details and how to add them to your urban structures.

Windows and Doors

Most building kits and modules come with cast window sashes and clear plastic for glass. However, if you simply glue plain glass behind the windows, the structure will look pretty empty. In actuality, windows in office buildings or shops that face the street usually have signs painted on them with the name of the business or the products and services offered. Main Street Graphics makes a line of printed windows for many of the more popular urban structure kits on the market today. These windows are manufactured to line up with the window openings of the kit, so that an entire wall full of windows can be installed at once. Figure 5-12 shows an example of these window signs installed in a City Classics Iron Front building. Main Street Graphics also offers windows with curtains, venetian blinds, and shades for use in side or rear windows, as well as the windows of modular building components. Walthers makes decals for signs that can be used in storefront windows of many of their Cornerstone urban structures and offers window material with preprinted venetian blinds on them.

In many older brick structures, a window or door is no longer used. In the case of a window, the sash is usually removed entirely, and bricks close in color to the outside wall are used to seal the window opening. Older brick factories used external beam hoists to lift loads to work areas on upper stories. Workers would lean out a door in the wall, and pull the load inside— a dangerous proposition. When external elevator shafts were added to these buildings, the old doors were bricked over. Modeling bricked-up windows and doors is simple. Take a scrap piece of brick (it doesn't have to be an exact match to the bricks in the structure's walls), and cut it to fit the opening. Then paint it a reasonable match to the color of the building (a little lighter or darker is fine), add mortar, and glue it into the opening (see fig. 5-13).

Fire Escapes

One of the most visible details on urban structures built prior to the mid-1930s is the external fire escape. While some kits come with fire escapes, more often they are overlooked and must be added. Fire escape kits are available from companies that specialize in detail parts for

5-12

5-13

buildings, including Model Memories and SS Ltd. Model Memories makes a very realistic kit consisting of etched brass parts that can be cut to fit most urban structures. You can assemble the kit with gap-filling cyanoacrylate or by soldering. The best way to add a fire escape to one of your buildings is to build it on your workbench, separate from the structure, and then glue it place with cyanoacrylate (CA). Be sure to measure the window spacing and between floor dimensions of your structure first so that the fire escape will fit. Paint the completed fire escape before attaching it to the structure. Most fire escapes are black, but other colors are used, including brown or oxide red. After painting, add a thin coat of Rustall for weathering. If your completed fire escape has an angle on the inside that rests against the building's wall, it may be glued in place with cyanoacrylate. If it does not, drill no. 68 holes in the building wall at the ends of each landing as shown in fig. 5-14. Next, glue a piece of .030"-diameter brass wire in each hole, and cut the protruding portion $1/16$" shorter than the width of the landing (see fig. 5-14). Finally, glue

Fig. 5-12. Lettering on commercial building windows, such as the company name and services or products offered, is very common on older urban structures. Preprinted windows are available for many building kits, as shown in this photo. You can also use decals to achieve the same effect.

Fig. 5-13. These openings in the wall of a brick building were once windows. To get this effect, remove the sash and fill in the opening with brick slightly different in color. The black smudges around the opening (made with chalk) indicate there might have been a fire causing a wooden sash to burn.

the landings to the wire with cyanoacrylate (CA). Figure 5-15 shows a Model Memories fire escape on a structure built from DPM Modules.

Air Conditioners, Evaporators, and Blowers

Window air conditioners (or evaporators, as the early units were called) were a common sight on most urban structures built before the mid-1950s. The primary exceptions were large office buildings, which had central air installed after they were built and were retrofitted with rooftop, packaged, air-conditioning units. Model Masterpieces, Campbell, and IHC all make window air

Fig. 5-14. As shown in the drawing, you can attach a fire escape to the wall of a brick building by using .030″ brass wire support rods.

Fig. 5-15. An etched-brass fire escape has been added to the outside of this building. External fire escapes are very common in cities, and the delicate etched railings look very much like the wrought-iron prototype.

Fig. 5-16. Window air conditioners began to appear on older urban buildings in the late 1940s and are available as detail parts. The small unit at the upper left cools an executive's office, while the large unit at the lower right handles a conference room or work area.

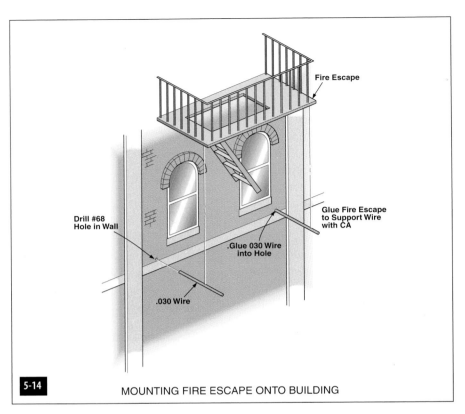

5-14

MOUNTING FIRE ESCAPE ONTO BUILDING

conditioners, which you must assemble, paint, and glue into the window frames (see fig. 5-16). Window air conditioners usually came in three colors, tan (Polly Scale Earth), green (½ Polly Scale Milwaukee Gray, ½ Signal Green), and gray (Polly Scale CP Gray). Most units made prior to 1970 had a brace on each side that ran at a 45° angle from the wall of the building under the window to the back of the air conditioner, which stuck out of the window.

A similar piece of detail, quite common on industrial buildings, was a window- or wall-mounted exhaust blower. It consisted of an enclosed fan with a vertical exhaust pipe. The unit was mounted on the building's wall outside a room that needed special ventilation. SS Ltd. makes a well-detailed exhaust blower kit consisting of metal castings. Assemble them with cyanoacrylate (CA) cement, and then mount the blower outside a window or a wall. A patch of metal served as a bulkhead where the blower duct went through the wall or window. You can easily make the patch from .010″ sheet styrene. Many of these blowers were connected to an exhaust stack that ran up the side of the building, protruded above the roof line, and was topped with a sheet-metal cap.

Here's how to install an exhaust blower in one of the structures on the urban railroad module. Start by

5-15

5-16

assembling the SS Ltd. blower kit, following the instructions. Paint it Polly Scale Tarnished Black with a light coat of Rustall for weathering. Cement the assembly to the brick wall of the building with cyanoacrylate, and add two braces made from .020″ x .020″ styrene below it. Use a scrap piece of round sprue from a plastic kit as an exhaust chimney. Its diameter should be the same size as the blower's exhaust pipe. Cut the sprue to length so that it ends about ½″ below the roof line, paint it

Tarnished Black, and cement it to the wall. Finally, glue a plastic stack with a cap (from a Grandt Line Engine House Stack Set) on top of the sprue so that it protrudes ½″ above the roof line. The completed blower and stack are shown in fig. 5-17.

What's on the Roof

From a detail standpoint, the roof of most city structures built prior to 1950 was the most complicated part of the structure. After 1950, many of the roof vents, stacks, and exhaust

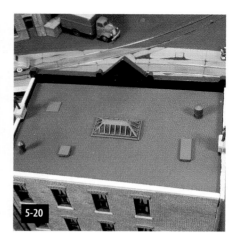

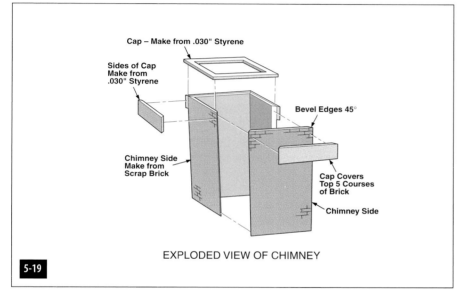

Cap – Make from .030" Styrene

Sides of Cap
Make from
.030" Styrene

Bevel Edges 45°

Chimney Side
Make from
Scrap Brick

Cap Covers
Top 5 Courses
of Brick

Chimney Side

EXPLODED VIEW OF CHIMNEY

5-19

Fig. 5-17. You can add an exhaust blower and its vertical stack to an older city structure after it is built. The blower and stack cap are available as detail parts. Make the vertical stack from a plastic casting sprue.

Fig. 5-18. The rooftops on the Sheas' module (Chapter 2) show a variety of skylights, stacks, and vents. There is an abundance of detail parts that can give urban rooftops the cluttered look of the prototype.

Fig. 5-19. Build brick or concrete chimneys of any size using the techniques shown in this drawing.

Fig. 5-20. The rectangular hatches on the left and right sides of this building's roof provide trap door access to the roof and its vents and stacks. Hatches like these are very common on smaller city buildings.

fans were enclosed in a rooftop machine room, whose walls and roof looked like an extension of the building below it. In this section we'll look at the many types of roof details which cluttered the roofs of older buildings; however, the arrangement of these details on any given roof was unique, and is up to you.

Chimneys

Every city building has some kind of heating plant whose exhaust is released into the air through one or more chimneys. Chimneys were usually the same material as the building (brick or concrete) and extended anywhere from 5 to 15 feet above the roof. There are exceptions to this rule of thumb, and tall tapered chimneys

up to 100 feet can be found in urban areas on power plants and factories. Most rooftop chimneys were brick, ranging in size from 2 x 2 feet to 10 x 10 feet.

While the top of many chimneys was just an open flue leading down to the heating plant, others had metal pipes above them, which were topped by a cap above the brick to keep rain (and pigeons) out of the hot exhaust smoke. Conical sheet-metal caps as well as T-shaped metal chimneys with angled exhaust pipes were all used and are available from detail parts manufacturers. Figure 5-18 shows several different types of metal and masonry chimney.

A number of manufacturers, among them SS Ltd., Campbell,

Alexander, and Grandt Line make small chimneys that are suitable for buildings up to two to three stories tall. Larger chimneys (6 to 10 feet square) are usually available only as part of a complete structure kit.

To build large brick chimneys for the modular buildings of the urban railroad in Chapter 4, use scrap wall modules and strip styrene. After determining the size of the chimney—length, width, and height—cut its four sides from a scrap brick module. Then bevel the inner edges of each side at a 45° angle to leave an unbroken brick surface on the outside. Glue the four sides together to form a square or rectangle and allow it to dry. Then make the chimney cap by first gluing four side pieces of

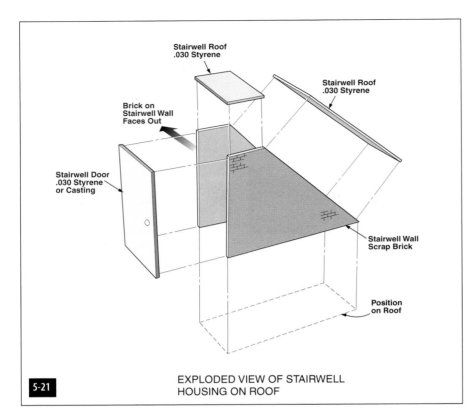

Stairwell Roof
.030 Styrene

Stairwell Roof
.030 Styrene

Brick on
Stairwell Wall
Faces Out

Stairwell Door
.030 Styrene
or Casting

Stairwell Wall
Scrap Brick

Position
on Roof

5-21

EXPLODED VIEW OF STAIRWELL
HOUSING ON ROOF

Fig. 5-21. Build a brick or concrete roof stairwell housing using the techniques shown in this drawing.

several detail parts manufacturers) across the vertical end of the wall pieces. Next, cut two pieces of roof from .030″ styrene, one to cover the top of the wall before the slope, the second to cover the slope to the roof. Assemble the walls, door, and roof as shown in fig. 5-21 with plastic cement, and paint the walls the same color as the building. The door and roof pieces should be painted Grimy Black. Add some Mortar Wash no. 1 to the brick. When it's dry, glue the walls to the roof. Figure 5-22 shows a roof stairwell in the upper left of the picture.

Vents and Coolers

Buildings built before central air-conditioning and environmental control had a number of vents on the roof that removed hot air from upper stories, fumes from commercial and manufacturing businesses, and stale air from lofts. Several types of vents commonly found on the roofs of urban buildings include:

• Mushroom vents. Shaped like the top of a mushroom, these contained a fan that pulled air from the inside of the building. The mushroom dome served as a cover to keep rain, snow, birds, and vermin out of the mechanism. Figure 5-22 shows a pair of mushroom vents near the front of the roof.

• Globe vents were fans whose blades, rather than lying flat, were vertical and shaped like a crescent. The blades were very close together, giving the vent the appearance of a sphere, or globe. Globe vents had two advantages: first, they did not need to turn at a high speed because there were many blades; and second, their shape did not require a cap to keep the elements out. Figure 5-22 shows two large globe vents along the center line of the building.

.030″ strip styrene to the outside of the chimney, covering the top three lines of brick. Next, cut a top from .030″ styrene with its outer dimensions matching those of the chimney top, and an inner hole 18 scale inches smaller in each dimension.

Paint the body of the chimney the same color as the brick of the building and add a coat of Mortar Wash no. 1 to the brick. When this is dry, paint the inside flue flat black and the cap concrete. Complete the chimney by drybrushing black chalk dust onto the cap and about a third of the way down the chimney walls. Glue the finished chimney to the roof with plastic cement. Figure 5-19 shows a typical chimney assembly.

Access Stairways and Hatches

There are two ways to get onto the roof of a city building. Smaller buildings (three stories or less) usually have a trap door, which is raised from the inside by standing on a ladder and then climbing onto the roof. Larger buildings have an extra flight of stairs leading onto the roof through a sloped enclosure with a door in it called a stairwell housing.

The simplest trap door is a piece of .030″ sheet styrene that is cut in a square or rectangle. (The smallest practical opening is 3 x 3 feet.) Also, Design Preservation Models makes a roof detail kit that includes several different sizes of hatches ready to glue in place. Paint these hatches Polly Scale Tarnished Black with a light coat of Rustall to age them. Figure 5-20 shows some roof hatches in place.

There are no kits on the market for a stairwell access to a roof, but they are easy to make. From a scrap piece of modular brick, cut two triangular walls 8 scale feet along the bottom and 6½ scale feet high at the end with a 2-scale-foot-long flat area on the top between the end and the beginning of the slope back to the roof (see fig. 5-21). These parts must be mirror images with the brick facing outward. Cement a solid door (made from scrap .030″ styrene sheet) or a panel door (available from

Fig. 5-22. This large market building has a stairwell in the upper left-hand corner of the roof that allows access to the equipment on the roof's surface. In the upper right, there is a rooftop cooler whose fan and ductwork must be serviced regularly.

Fig. 5-23. Model city roofs can be very realistic. The red brick buildings across the center have a clutter of vents, stacks, and skylights. Note the electrified "Hotel" sign on the roof of the beige building at left.

• Cylinder vents looked like a can with a conical top. While some of these contained fans, others worked by convection, allowing heat from dead air spaces (such as the peaks on loft buildings) to rise and exhaust through the vent to the outside of the structure. The buildings in figs. 5-18 and 5-22 have two cylinder vents each between their skylights.

• Stacks provided a vent for the interior plumbing of a building so that waste water could flow into the city's sewers without smelly bubbles rising through the pipes and toilets. They are functionally like the stack above your house's drains. Stacks were metal pipes that stuck up through the roof and often had conical metal caps on them to prevent blockage by snow or birds. Figures 5-18 and 5-23 show a variety of stacks on building roofs.

• Roof-mounted blowers were used where large amounts of air or fumes had to be exhausted from a building. These were larger versions of the wall-mounted blowers de-scribed in an earlier section of this chapter and were used to exhaust a number of rooms or an entire building. A roof blower is located at the right rear of the structure in fig. 5-22.

• Coolers were refrigeration units placed on the roofs of older commercial buildings that had a number of refrigerated cold rooms. These were boxlike structures with a number of fans visible from their top surface. Figure 5-24 shows a close up of a rooftop cooler on the Mass Bay Fish Market (described in Chapter 4).

Fortunately for the city modeler, there is a good selection of different-size vent castings in plastic, metal, and urethane from a number of manufacturers. There is also a kit for a 20-ton rooftop cooler made by Alloy Forms, which can also be used as a packaged building air-conditioning unit.

I usually paint roof vents Polly Scale Tarnished Black or Pacemaker Gray with a coat of Rustall, as most vents were made of sheet metal and tended to rust between paint jobs. The exceptions are the newer globe vents, which were made of aluminum after the mid-1930s. I paint these with Floquil Old Silver covered with a black wash (30:1 dilution) or a light coat of Rustall. For a rooftop cooler, I use Polly Scale CP Gray, with the fans painted Tarnished Black. I add a light coat of Rustall to the cooler's enclosure and a heavier coat to its fans.

Skylights

Skylights were prevalent on older city structures and provided light to stairwells and top-floor work areas during daylight hours. Campbell makes a styrene kit for a skylight; when used singly, it is the right size for a stairwell, and in multiples it can be used to light work areas. Paint the walls, ends, and window dividers Tarnished Black before gluing the clear sections in place. If you use a fast-drying plastic cement like Tenax 7R you will not harm the paint. Figure 5-18 shows four of these skylights in place on a roof. Larger skylights, made of etched brass—both square and rectangular—are available from Model Memories. You'll have to bend the parts to shape and glue or solder the seams together before installing the glass. If you choose to solder the parts, make sure that you first remove all of the varnish from the surface of the brass parts with lacquer thinner, or the solder will not adhere.

Before attaching a brass skylight to the roof, build a frame made from .030″ x .030″ styrene strip and glue it around the base of the skylight with cyanoacrylate (CA). The strips provide a surface thick enough to adhere to the roof (the brass is very thin), and duplicates weather stripping found on the prototype. While they are more time-consuming to build than plastic skylights, these brass skylights are fine pieces of detail, worth

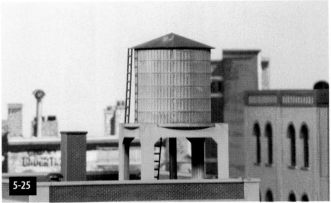

Fig. 5-24. A rooftop cooler at the rear center of the roof of the Mass Bay Fish Market refrigerates a cold room on the top floor. Market buildings like this often had coolers on the roof, added after the structure was built.

Fig. 5-25. Water towers are very common on city buildings over four stories high. This wooden tank, which sits on a concrete base, came with the building kit.

Fig. 5-26. Build a rooftop water tank, currently only available as part of a structure kit, using the techniques shown in this drawing.

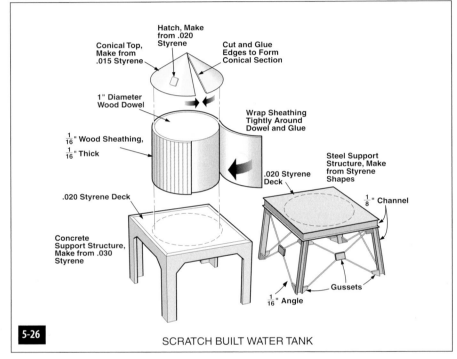

SCRATCH BUILT WATER TANK

Water Tanks

Water tanks were mounted on the roofs of city buildings six stories or higher and served as reservoirs for a building. Water was pumped up to the tank to keep it full. When needed by occupants, it flowed down into the building by gravity. Water tanks were usually made of wood or steel plates and supported above the roof by concrete or structural steel legs.

Paint the body of a wood water tower with Floquil Earth and then give it a coat of Black Mortar Wash no. 2 to pick out the scribing between the wood. If the tank is of metal construction, paint it Tarnished Black, with a light coat of Rustall for weathering. Next paint the conical top of the tank Grimy Black, followed by the support structure—Tarnished Black if it is steel, Aged Concrete if it is made of concrete. Then assemble

the parts. Finally, add some additional weathering with chalks, which includes some vertical streaks of light brown to the tank to simulate rain run-off, and white streaks to the roof to simulate bird refuse. Figure 5-25 shows a closeup of a wooden water tower on a concrete base.

While a number of urban and industrial building kits include roof water tanks, I could find only two made as detail parts (and one of these is often in short supply). Art Curren, author of several books on kitbashing structures, once told me to buy kits with water towers when they are on sale at shows—just to get the water

tower. This is good advice (if the price is right). An alternate is to scratchbuild one. The starting point is a piece of wood dowel 1" in diameter. This is a good size for HO; use a larger size for S and O scale. Cut it to a height of 15 scale feet. Moisten and then carefully wrap a piece of $\frac{1}{16}$" scribed wood around the dowel, and cut it so the ends meet. Attach this wrapper to the dowel with a good contact cement such as Goo and hold it in place with rubber bands until dry. Make the conical top from .015" styrene, cut in a circle whose diameter is about $\frac{1}{8}$" greater than the tank and wrapper. Remove a small pie-

the extra effort. A large brass skylight appears in fig. 5-20.

shaped wedge, and glue the ends together to form a shallow cone. It is a good idea to cement a piece of styrene under the joint to add strength. The base of the tank consists of a .030″ platform supported on legs made from .030″ styrene (concrete supports) or from styrene structural shapes (steel supports). Glue the top to the tank, and the tank to the support base. Add a piece of ⅛″-diameter brass tubing between the bottom of the tank and the roof to simulate the water pipe running into the building. When it's dry, cement the completed water tank to the roof. Finally, add a piece of ladder from the roof to the top of the tank for cleaning and inspection. Figure 5-26 shows the tank's assembly.

Roof Surface

Most flat city roofs were covered with tar to provide a weather seal. Spray roofs with Floquil Grimy Black (a good match for tar) before adding any details. After the details are in place, draw in seams and patches with a short straightedge and a Micron marking pen with a no. 005 extra-fine tip. If you like, add some white specks (from birds) by stippling white chalk dust onto the roof with a stiff-bristled brush, removing any excess chalk with a vacuum.

An alternate roof surface, one usually found on older brick structures, is a fine gravel with tar underneath. To simulate, first install the roof on the structure and cement all roof details in place. For the gravel use fine black ballast or cinders one scale smaller than that which you are modeling. (If the building is HO, use N scale ballast.) Spread a thin layer of ballast, and gently pat it down until it is level. Next, gently cover the gravel with a very fine spray of "wet water" from a pump bottle held at a distance so that no heavy drops splash and make holes in the gravel layer. Wipe the water off any roof details with a soft

cloth, and then drop Woodland Scenics Scenic Cement carefully onto the gravel from an eye-dropper held very near the surface of the gravel. The cement dries flat and holds the gravel in place. A good example of a gravel roof is shown in fig. 5-18.

Signs

Most city structures have signs on their walls or roofs to identify the type of building (warehouse, hotel, etc.) or advertise products. These signs usually fall into three categories:

• Signs painted on a wall of the building.

• Freestanding signs mounted on the front of the structure facing the street.

• Rooftop signs—billboards, neon signs, or electric signs.

Painted Wall Signs

Signs painted on the brick or concrete outer surface of a building range in complexity from simple letters to advertising graphics. You can make all-letter signs from dry-transfer alphabet sets, available in a number of typefaces, sizes, and colors from Woodland Scenics. The first step is to decide whether the sign should have a colored background or a border, typical of many urban signs dating from the 1920s to the 1940s. Figure 5-27 shows such a sign on the Atlantic Warehouse building shown in the lead photo to this chapter. Here's how to make it.

Start by selecting the color of the sign (in this case yellow letters on a black background) and determining its size. Lay out the sign on a piece of paper, using the dry-transfer letters and a scale ruler to keep the letters straight. Draw a rectangle around the letters and write down its dimensions. Then put masking tape around a section of brick wall that matches these dimensions. Spray the brick where the sign will go Flat Black; when the paint is dry, remove the

masking tape. Add a piece of ¹⁄₃₂″ white chart tape under where each line of text will go. Spell out each line of text on a pad of paper, count the total number of letters and spaces, and divide it by two to obtain the center of the line. Starting with the center letter (or space), apply yellow dry-transfer letters one by one, first from the center to the end of the line, and then backwards from the center to the beginning of the line. The horizontal tape under the line ensures that the line of letters is straight. If you have to remove a letter, pull it off gently with a small piece of masking tape. Remove the ¹⁄₃₂″ tape and add a border using ¹⁄₁₆″ yellow dry-transfer striping. When the sign is complete, lay the dry-transfer backing sheet over it and rub a burnishing tool over the letters and into the spaces between the bricks. The final step is to drybrush a little yellow chalk dust below each letter for weathering.

Wall signs advertising products are more complicated, since they require graphics or pictures. There are three ways of mounting these on buildings:

• Glue on a paper ad. George Sellios and several manufacturers of period advertisements recommend gluing a full-color ad printed on paper to the building. The first step is to lightly buff the face of the paper ad with steel wool to age it. Next, sand the back of the ad gently using very fine sandpaper or emery cloth to make the paper as thin as possible. Then apply a thin coat of white glue to the back of the paper with a fingertip, and immediately place the ad on the wall, glue side down. Press the ad into place, and smooth it down from the center to the edges to eliminate bubbles. You can run a fingernail gently along the lines of brick to make the paper snuggle down into the mortar lines. Finally, use a damp cloth to wipe away any excess glue that has oozed onto the surrounding brick. While this technique can be messy

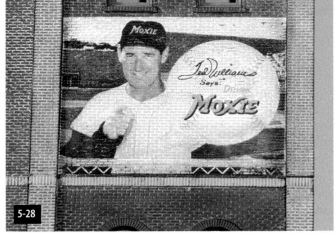

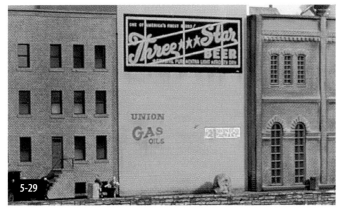

Fig. 5-27. Until the advent of modern glass high-rise buildings, signs were either painted or pasted on the walls of most commercial city buildings. Make the "Atlantic Market" sign by painting a portion of the brick wall black and adding yellow dry-transfer lettering over it.

Fig. 5-28. This wall advertisement of Ted Williams of the Boston Red Sox endorsing Moxie, a favorite soft drink of Boston residents, is typical of advertisements on the walls of urban buildings. This sign is a decal, applied with plenty of solvent so the brickwork shows through it.

Fig. 5-29. The "Three Star Beer" ad on the wall of this beige building is a dry transfer. By burnishing the transfer in place, the lines of the brick will show through.

and takes a little practice, it works well and has the advantage of using real ads cut from old magazines.

• Decals. Several companies make full-color ads on decal paper, including Microscale and Art Griffin (mail order: 2734 Floral Trail, Michigan City, IN 46360). On one of the structures on the Union Freight module (Chapter 4), I decided to use one of Griffin's ads from the 1940s showing Ted Williams—of Boston Red Sox fame—endorsing Moxie, a popular local soft drink (see fig. 5-28). To use one of these ads, start by dipping the decal in water for 45 seconds. Before sliding it onto the structure, apply a coating of decal solvent (Champ Decal Set, Walthers SolvaSet, Microscale Microset, etc.) onto the brick of structure, and slide the decal off the paper and onto the wall. After positioning the decal, apply another coat of solvent on top of the wet decal. After a few minutes, as the decal film softens, pop any trapped air bubbles using the point of a no. 11 blade in a hobby knife, and gently work the decal film into the mortar lines. Repeat this process twice, until all of the brickwork shows through. When the decal has dried overnight, brush a coat of Black Mortar Wash no. 1 over it to highlight the individual bricks. When using the alcohol-based wash, be careful to make sure it does not fade the darker decal inks or cause them to run. (If this starts to happen, gently wipe the wash off with a damp cloth.) As a final step, spray the decal with Dullcote to eliminate any highlights.

• Dry transfers. Woodland Scenics, Clover House, and Vintage Reproductions all make dry-transfer ads. Apply them by placing them over the wall and rubbing them until all of the ad is on the wall. Fix the ad in place by placing the backing paper over it and burnishing it in place. Pick out the mortar lines by gently running a fingernail into the crack through the backing paper. Weather dry-transfer ads using chalk dust and a stiff-bristled brush. Figure 5-29 shows a building with several dry-transfer ads on its walls.

Freestanding Signs

Many storefront city buildings have signs (painted and neon) mounted on their walls facing the street. These signs identify the shops—their names and what they sell—to pedestrians. Walthers makes a kit of plastic signs in different shapes that come with decals to fit the signs. The user must paint the sign, apply the decals, and glue it to

Fig. 5-30. While rooftop billboards look complex, they are easy to build from plastic structural shapes, using the construction techniques shown in this drawing.

Fig. 5-31. Like billboards, rooftop electric signs are easy to build from plastic structural shapes and vinyl letters, using the construction techniques shown in this drawing.

the front of the building. If you want words other than those on the decals, you can use an alphabet set—either dry transfers or decals—to customize the sign for your building. The lead photo in Chapter 4 shows one of these freestanding signs on a building roof.

Rooftop Signs

Depending on the height and the message being conveyed, two kinds of rooftop signs were popular on city buildings—billboards and electric or neon signs. Let's look at some examples of each.

Roof billboards consisted of full-color paper signs mounted on a steel frame. They were used on buildings two to five stories high and almost always lighted by floodlights on the roof or in front of the sign. Build roof billboards starting with an HO advertisement, available from a number of vendors. After cutting out the ad, make a backplate from .020" styrene cut to the same size. Depending on the billboard's width, make four or five equally spaced vertical support members from 1/16" styrene channel and cement them to the rear of the backplate. Cut these vertical supports to reach from the roof's surface to the top of the billboard, making sure that the bottom of the billboard is at least 6 feet above the roof. That way it can be seen by pedestrians without the roof blocking the view. Then cut a second set of styrene channels and glue them to the support legs sloping 30° to the rear. Finally, add cross bracing made from 1/16" angle across the front and back of the vertical and angled sup-

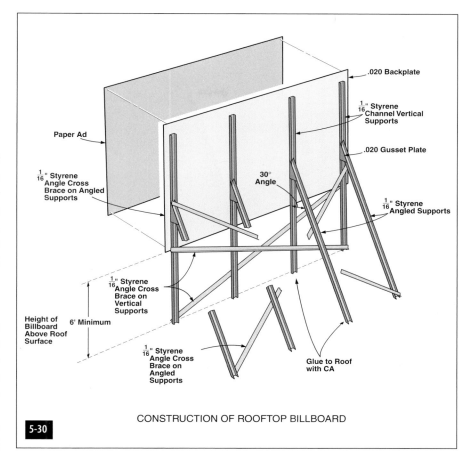

CONSTRUCTION OF ROOFTOP BILLBOARD

5-30

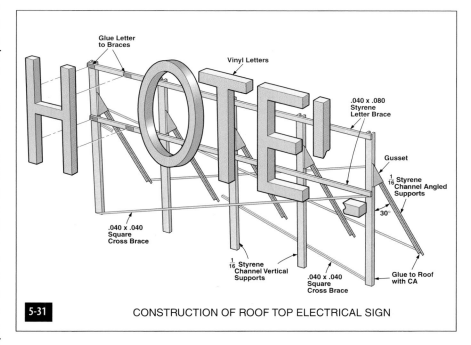

CONSTRUCTION OF ROOF TOP ELECTRICAL SIGN

5-31

port members. Figure 5-30 shows typical billboard construction.

Paint the assembly Polly Scale Tarnished Black. The last step is to glue the sign to the backplate. Coat the back of the sign with 3M no. 77 spray adhesive and mount it very carefully on the plastic backplate. Apply finger pressure first on the center of the sign and then move to the

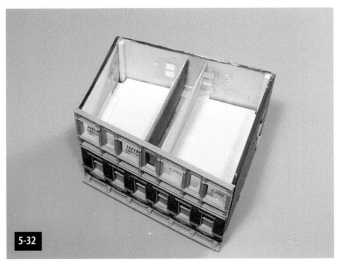

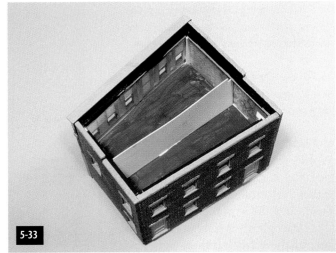

Fig. 5-32. Sheet styrene partitions running front to back on the ground floor of this building prevent a viewer from looking in a side window and seeing out a window on the other side of the building. The partitions also define a store space if you want to detail the inside of the structure.

Fig. 5-33. A single styrene partition running the length of the top floor of this building prevents you from looking through the structure. The floor, also made of styrene, is painted brown to simulate wood.

edges. This eliminates any air bubbles that could get trapped under the sign. Then put a drop of gap-filling cyano-acrylate on the ends of the support members and glue them to the roof.

Electric and neon signs usually consist of words (such as HOTEL) or a company logo. They are lighted either by neon tubes or from the inside through a translucent shell. These highly visible signs are found on taller buildings of ten stories or more. Quality Products Co. makes a variety of working electric sign kits that are suitable for rooftop use.

If you do not need a sign to actually light up, you can build one using the same techniques as you used for a billboard. Start by building a support structure similar to a billboard's. However, instead of a solid plastic back plate, run two horizontal stringers made from .040″ x 080″ styrene strip to hold the letters and glued to the

vertical supports. You can buy vinyl letters from a graphic arts supply shop. They come in sizes ranging from ¼″ to 2″ and are available in a variety of colors. Glue the letters to the stringers to form the word(s) you want, and then cement the support frame to the roof. Figure 5-31 shows the construction of a rooftop electric sign.

Additional tips on detailing structures can be found in Art Curren's book, *Kitbashing HO Model Railroad Structures*, which is published by Kalmbach Books and available at most hobby shops. While Art's book deals with industrial and railroad structures as well as urban buildings, his detailing tips complement those described above.

Building Interiors

We all have a special structure that we have superdetailed inside and out—a station, a roundhouse, an interlocking tower, etc. Think of the time and effort that went into that one structure, and then multiply it by 100—that is the amount of effort you would have to put into a city to add interior details to most of the buildings. The work is mind-boggling.

A good compromise for the urban modeler is to add simple interior partitions and floors to city buildings. These prevent a visitor from looking through a building and seeing out the

windows of several stories on the other side, or looking into a storefront window and seeing other empty stores on each side. Below are some rules of thumb to consider when adding interior partitions to urban structures.

Floors

I add floors inside multistory structures as visual barriers so you can't see out of the windows of several stories on the other side. Make floors from .020″ sheet styrene and support them on ¼″ styrene angles glued to the walls at each floor. Paint the top surface of the floor black, dark gray, or dark brown to simulate wood or office carpeting.

Partitions

Add partitions running from the front to back of a structure to separate the stores on the ground floor of the building. This makes each store appear as a self-contained unit (like the prototype). Paint these partitions in pastel shades—ivory, light yellow, light green, etc.—to make each store look a little different when viewed from the street. Figure 5-32 shows the partitions separating two stores and a stairwell (in the center) in a DPM building underneath. On the second story and those above it run a single partition along the length of the structure, to prevent the viewer from look-

5-34

Fig. 5-34. Carefully designed street and building lights help create dramatic city scenes like this one on Al Kubicka's HO scale Panhandle Route.

ing in the front and out the back of the building. The partition does not have to run the entire length of the structure; different-length partitions add variety. Leave this partition white to look like a plastered interior wall. Figure 5-33 shows such a longitudinal partition painted white; the floor beneath it is brown. (The roof has been removed from the structure.)

While the interior floors and partitions described above are used as visual barriers in urban structures, there are also opportunities to selectively superdetail a few rooms in structures that a viewer can easily see. The structure that contains one or more detailed rooms should be either on an aisle with windows easy to look into or a few inches from the edge of the city, perhaps at the end of an alley, which serves as a visual pathway to the structure.

Lighting Your City

Since I run my trains with the cellar lights on (i.e., daytime operation),

I do not have working lights in my city structures. However, many modelers spend as much effort to light their cities as they do to build them. John Allen, one of the legendary names in the hobby, had an electromechanical system to simulate the passage of an entire day and night on his Gorre and Daphetid. All the lights on and over his layout were controlled by a large cylinder that looked like a giant music box drum. As it turned slowly, pins on the cylinder's surface triggered lights all over the railroad and simulated the sun rising in the east, moving across the sky, and setting in the west.

At twilight, blue bulbs heralded the onset of night, and the lights on the streets and in buildings of John's large city, called Port, came on for a dramatic effect. He even used ultraviolet lights and fluorescent paint for neon signs.

Since John Allen's pioneering work in the 1960s, the technology has changed greatly. Electronics based on

integrated circuit chips now do the same work as his mechanical drum in a fraction of the space and for less cost. Nighttime city lighting is a subject in itself and is beyond the scope of this book.

Here are three key articles on city lighting that have appeared in recent years:

- "Some Tips on Interior Lighting," by John Wesner, *Model Railroader* magazine, November 1983
- "Modeling High Rise Buildings," by Mike Palmiter, *Model Railroader* magazine, August 1992
- "Lighting the Great Western Railroad," by Bob Boelter, *Model Railroader* magazine, March 1996
- "Lighting for Realism," by Gregory H. Heier, *Model Railroader* magazine, December 1999

If you would like to light your city, you can get started by obtaining copies of these articles from *Model Railroader* magazine, 21027 Crossroads Circle, Waukesha, WI 53187.

A city is more than buildings and streets. Vehicles, people, and clutter are the things that make a city live. Think of how dull and lifeless this scene would be without the trucks, truck drivers, workers, trash cans, and crates on the loading docks.

DETAILING A CITY
CHAPTER 6

Cars, Trucks, People, and Junk

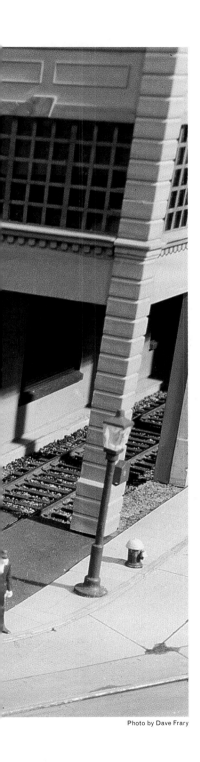

Photo by Dave Frary

S o far we have covered the design, construction, and detailing of the primary elements of a city: buildings, streets, bridges, and other significant structures. In this chapter we will look at all those details that make the streets and alleys come alive—vehicles, people, trash, and junk. We'll discuss what is available and how to make these details look realistic.

Fig. 6-1. This photo of Broadway in New York City was taken on a spring morning in 1958. The traffic consists of cars parked and moving, a taxi, and a bus. There are a few pedestrians on the sidewalk and a shopkeeper talking to a customer. You do not need a lot of vehicles and people to make a main city thoroughfare look real.

Fig. 6-2. In residential areas, as in this 1960 picture of a New York side street, traffic is very light. Most cars are parked with only one or two moving vehicles per block. The few pedestrians are going to or from work or talking with neighbors, and children are playing on the sidewalk—or in the case of stickball, in the street.

Fig. 6-3. Downtown commercial or market truck terminals had lots of activity. In this view of the Providence, Rhode Island, rail transfer station in the late 1930s, workmen were busy loading and unloading trucks, while drivers relaxed for a few minutes. There were plenty of crates, sacks of produce, and trash barrels to add to the clutter on the loading dock.

Vehicles

While city thoroughfares are used by automobiles, trucks, buses, parked cars, delivery vans, and taxicabs, the traffic on streets located in different parts of a city varies greatly. On a main avenue running through a residential or business district, you find mostly cars with a few buses and trucks. The curbs are lined with parked cars and perhaps an occasional delivery van (see fig. 6-1). On a residential side street, most vehicles are parked cars and only one or two moving cars or taxis may be visible (see fig. 6-2). In a city's older industrial or market districts, trucks predominate with lines of trailers sitting on their "landing gear" at loading docks being packed or unloaded (see fig. 6-3). There are more trucks waiting to maneuver into position. What cars are visible are usually parked. However, since the mid 1960s, when most cities modernized and rebuilt their centers, many of these industrial and market areas have been relocated to the suburbs, and the freight terminals with their crowded commercial traffic are beginning to vanish from the downtown scene.

Therefore, the mix of vehicles on your urban streets will depend both on the district of the city and the period that you are modeling. If your city depicts the period from the mid-1960s through the present, the majority of your vehicles will consist of cars, cabs, delivery vans, and buses. Most large trucks have been banished to suburban freight terminals, and those tractor-trailers that are on the streets are usually passing through. There is an excellent selection of HO vehicles available for this modern period from two groups of manufacturers:

• American Manufacturers—Atlas, Athearn, A-Line, Alloy Forms, Con-Cor, Ertl, IHC, Lonestar, On-Trak, Rail Power Products, and Trucks-N-Stuff (to name a few) make a wide range of vehicles from the 1960s to the '90s that will fit right into a modern cityscape.

• European Manufacturers—Busch, Eko, Herpa, Kibri, Pirate Models, Roco, Trident, and Wiking are all adding U.S. prototype vehicles to their existing European product lines. In addition, an increasing number of European vehicles—Volvo, Volkswagen, Mercedes-Benz,

6-4

6-5

6-6

Fig. 6-4. The traffic on this busy street consists of out-of-the-box modern vehicles. Note the shiny bodies and chrome, somewhat incompatible with a dirty thoroughfare in the heart of the city.

Fig. 6-5. Here are three Busch pickup trucks. The one on the left is out of box, with bright body and chrome. To duplicate the center truck, give the chrome and pickup bed a wash of india ink and paint its tires Grimy Black. To make the right-hand truck, dull the chrome, paint the tires, and also disassemble the truck and repaint the body with a flat acrylic. Notice how the realism increases with weathering.

Fig. 6-6. This is the same street as fig. 6-4, but now the traffic consists of cars and trucks of the late 1940s. The mix of flat, semigloss, and glossy finishes differentiates the old from new, as well as trucks from cars. Since all of these vehicles are from unpainted kits, the variation in color and finish is up to the builder.

Saab, etc.—have become common sights on today's U.S. city streets.

The vehicles from these vendors are made of highly detailed, injection-molded plastic or cast metal. They are sold painted and either assembled or as simple kits. The fact that these vehicles are complete saves you the time of painting—and sometimes even assembling—each truck and car. Figure 6-4 shows a group of modern vehicles out of the box.

Most of the U.S.-made trucks have silver-colored plastic for chrome parts, and their bodies are painted with a flat finish. European-made vehicles, on the other hand, have very bright chrome, and their colors are quite shiny. Some weathering will make them look more realistic. The simplest form of weather-

ing is to paint all of the chrome parts with a black wash of india ink diluted with 30 parts alcohol. Paint the tires Polly Scale Grimy Black and the visible, unpainted black plastic parts on the trucks Tarnished Black. If the vehicle is too shiny (as in the case of most trucks) tone down the bodies with Testors Dullcote applied with an airbrush. However, if the vehicle has clear windows, the Dullcote will give them a frosted look, depending on how much is applied. A solution is to disassemble the vehicle. Most of the plastic vehicles have press-fit parts, which you can separate by applying *gentle* pressure on the joints with a hobby knife or fine screwdriver. Do not use too much force, or you will break the parts. Once the vehicle is

in pieces, you can apply Dullcote to the colored parts. If you do not like the factory-supplied color, this also gives you a chance to repaint the body to suit your taste. Figure 6-5 shows examples of these different weathering techniques.

There are also modern vehicles (trucks, emergency vehicles, and construction equipment) that come as kits consisting of either cast metal or molded plastic parts. You'll have to glue them together, using cyanoacrylate (CA) for the metal kits and liquid plastic cement for the styrene ones, and then paint them. Paint these vehicle kits with Polly Scale flat acrylic colors to suit your taste. Use Grimy Black for the tires and Testors Chrome Silver enamel for the grille and trim. Once the paint

Fig. 6-7. A short-haul tractor transfers a meat trailer from a downtown market to a local warehouse. Such combinations were common city sights until markets and warehouses moved to the suburbs and modern, long-haul trucks became dominant in many areas of the United States.

Fig. 6-8. This 1940s city garbage truck was kitbashed from one manufacturer's cab and chassis, another vendor's body, and a third vendor's wheels. You can build virtually any kind of truck using this approach.

has dried, you can add a light spray of Glosscote from an airbrush to give the bodies some shine—the more shine, the newer-looking the vehicle.

If you model an earlier era, for example the 1940s (as I do), the availability of suitable cars, trucks, and buses is more limited. However, the supply is growing, and there are more vehicles from the 1920s, '30s and '40s on the market today than ever before. Most of the HO vehicles made for this period are kits consisting of cast resin or urethane, plaster, or metal parts that must be assembled and painted. To obtain a complete truck the modeler must often mix and match components, since one vendor may make the right cab and chassis, while another makes the right body. Figure 6-6 shows some of these period vehicles on the Union Freight module in Chapter 5.

Currently, a number of vendors make vehicle kits from the 1930s, '40s and '50s. These are listed below

with a brief description of their product lines.

• Stoney Mountain Castings makes over 70 HO car and truck models from 1936 to 1951. All parts are cast in urethane with sharp detail that is easy to paint. Some of the truck kits have front wheels that can be mounted straight or in a rotated position so the vehicle appears to be turning. The kits come with a color picture of the finished model to serve as a painting guide.

• Alloy Forms has about 50 cast metal car and truck kits from the 1940s and '50s (not including their more modern vehicles). The line includes such specialty items as fire trucks and emergency vehicles. The kits are well detailed, and the cars come with interiors and extras such as stick-on whitewalls for the tires.

• Greg's Garage lists 100 cars and trucks from the 1930s and '40s. The kits are cast in translucent resin, so you won't have to paint the windows. Automobiles make up about 85 percent of the line, and trucks come as cab and chassis with the bodies sold separately. You can use Greg's bodies with other vendors' chassis—good for kitbashing. Note that this manufacturer has only a few retail dealers, but does sell mail order from 911 Maple St., Saginaw, MI 48602.

• Jordan Products has about 20 vehicles, including Mack AC chain-drive trucks and fire engines, that

range from 1914 to the 1940s. The kits consist of delicate styrene parts and include painting guides and decals where appropriate.

• On-Trak has a highly detailed line of cast-metal trucks from the 1920s.

• Sheepscot Products manufacturers a growing line of 15 semi trailers and truck bodies cast in Hydrocal with metal hardware. These include 28-foot and 32-foot round-nose trailers, which were prevalent during the 1940s and early 1950s. Metal tractor kits are also available.

• Walthers manufacturers the former Magnuson line of cast urethane vehicles from the 1940s to the 1960s and has recently upgraded some of the kits so the bodies are hollow with open windows.

• Wheel Works makes cast metal truck and car kits from the early 1930s.

• Williams has a line of car kits from the 1920s to the '50s molded in clear styrene, which allows see-through windows in the bodies.

I used vehicles from most of these vendors on the cityscapes discussed in Chapters 2, 3, and 4. Assembling the kits is relatively straightforward and ranges from gluing wheels onto a cast body to gluing together a number of cast-metal or plastic components. Paint these kits as sub-assemblies: chassis, body, interior (if supplied), and wheels. Most prewar (1941) cars were painted black,

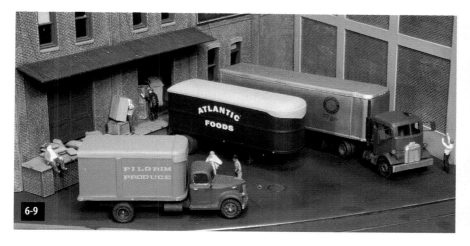

maroon, gray, or dark blue—colors that I remember from my youth in New York. Starting with the postwar models of the late 1940s, cars became brighter. There were many more colors to choose from, as well as two-tone schemes, in which the top and body were different colors. Trucks and trailers from this period were painted in a variety of colors including red, maroon, dark green, gray, and light or dark blue. They were lettered for both national and local carriers. Note that the roofs of the round-nosed trailers of the 1940s were usually light gray—Polly Scale Milwaukee Gray is a good match. Delivery vans could be found in all colors. Often bright shades of orange, yellow, and green were used to make the van stand out and advertise a delivery service or product. The techniques that I use to paint these period cars and trucks are described in my article "Painting Cast Resin Vehicles," which appeared in the January 1999 issue of *Model Railroader* (you can get copies by writing to *Model Railroader* magazine, 21027 Crossroads Circle, Waukesha, WI 53187).

I also kitbash the parts from several vendors to make specific period vehicles that I want, but that are not available as complete kits. Two examples include modeling tractor-trailers of the 1940s, and building specialty trucks. In the first example, moving trailers from downtown rail terminals to locations around a city was usually done by short-haul tractors, capable of handling a variety of different trailers—van, flatbed, tanker, etc. (Kalmbach's *The Model Railroader's Guide to Intermodal Equipment and Operations*, by Jeff Wilson, includes a list of available HO and N scale trailers appropriate for specific eras.) Figure 6-7 shows a stock Sheepscot 32-foot round-nosed meat trailer behind a short-haul, three-axle 1948 Sterling tractor, also from Sheepscot. The second example is a cab-over-engine garbage truck, quite common in the 1940s. Here, I used a Stoney Mountain 1938 SMC cab and chassis to which I glued a Greg's Garage garbage truck body. The result is shown in fig. 6-8.

Ultimately, the type and mix of city traffic is up to you. However, if you use the guidelines that are summarized below, your vehicles will make your city look very much like the prototype:

• Not every city street is clogged with moving traffic; the number of vehicles should match the use of the street.

• Vehicles found on city streets are readily available for the time period you model. You just have to know where to find them

• Virtually any city vehicle you need is either available complete or can be kitbashed from available parts.

Fig. 6-9. These workers are moving cargo from the loading dock to an inside receiving area in the Atlantic Market. Painting figures in work clothes appropriate to the season (it's late summer in the photo) and placing them in position to move crates adds to the realism of the urban scene.

Fig. 6-10. Even on the corner of a busy avenue, pedestrians talk and gossip. The owner of a bakery complains to a customer about the rising cost of flour, while two housewives share the news of the neighborhood. By arranging pedestrians in groups of two or three, you make them look natural.

Figures

I usually divide people for my cities into three groups:

• Workmen load and unload trucks in industrial and market areas, dig up streets in road repair crews, etc.

• Business people and tradespeople work in offices and stores, but can be found on the streets running errands, during lunch hour, or going to and from work.

• Pedestrians—housewives, children, and men—walk to stores and schools, talk on city sidewalks, or relax in backyards.

The chief differences between these three kinds of city dwellers are their postures (i.e., what they are doing) and their clothing. When selecting figures for your city scene, consider both of these factors.

Posture shows what the figure is doing. Workmen may be carrying crates to or from trucks on a loading

Fig. 6-11. This street scene has the look of the late 1940s from the Mercury Woody station wagon to the 1941 Chevy cab. The businessmen across the street are wearing hats, while the lady on the lower right carries paper bags of groceries home. If your cars and the clothes people wear match a given period, the city will match it too.

Fig. 6-12. This drawing shows the three simple steps that will make a standing figure lean against a crate.

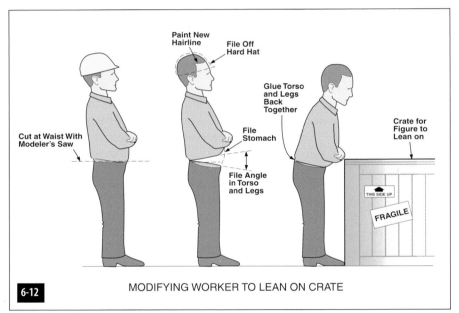

Paint New Hairline

File Off Hard Hat

Glue Torso and Legs Back Together

Cut at Waist With Modeler's Saw

File Stomach

File Angle in Torso and Legs

Crate for Figure to Lean on

THIS SIDE UP

FRAGILE

6-12   MODIFYING WORKER TO LEAN ON CRATE

for a housewife, shorts for a youngster. Workmen wear dark overalls or work-pants and work shirts or T-shirts. The season of the year also has an impact on clothing. In the fall or spring, sweaters and raincoats are common; while in the winter everyone wears a coat or heavy jacket. In the summer you may see workmen bare to the waist and pedestrians in shorts. Finally, you should consider the period that you are modeling for the style and color of its clothing. Figures 6-9 and 6-10 show a variety of late-1940s outfits on different figures.

A huge number of molded plastic figures are available in HO alone. The largest and best-detailed selection comes from Preiser (2000 figures), Merten (500 figures), and Noch (300 figures). All three firms are European, and while some of their figures have on local clothing (lederhosen/alpine hats, European railway uniforms, etc.), the majority look quite at home on a U.S. city street. These companies' figures come painted in packages of six to eight grouped by posture or function (women hanging wash, railroad passengers, people sitting, etc.) for prices ranging from $8.95 to $13.95 (average cost per figure: $1.75). Bachmann and Model Power also sell HO painted figures that are not as well detailed or painted but are available at a correspondingly lower price (average cost per figure: $1.00). In addition, Preiser sells most of its line of figures unpainted in bulk packages, 130 for $24.95 (average cost per figure: 19 cents).

dock or guiding a truck into the dock with hand signals. Members of a street repair gang may be digging up old pavement with a jackhammer or smoothing new asphalt with a shovel. A baker may be carrying a fresh load of bread in a basket, while a housewife may be pinning up wash to dry in a backyard. A businessman may be striding along the sidewalk with a briefcase, while two women are talking to each other just a few feet away. Each of these figures has a different posture that is unique to the task or activity that he

or she is performing, see fig. 6-9.

Clothing differs, depending on whether a figure is a businessman, worker, tradesperson, or pedestrian. Businessmen usually wear suits, coats (if the season dictates), and hats (if the scene is 1955 or earlier). Tradespeople often wear clothing or uniforms specific to their jobs. A baker wears a white shirt and pants, while a policeman or member of the armed forces wears a uniform. Pedestrians usually dress in casual clothes depending on sex and age—a T-shirt and jeans for a teenager, a sweater and skirt or slacks

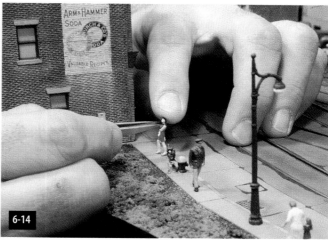

Out-of-the-box figures will meet the vast majority of your different posture needs (running, sitting, climbing stairs, handling crates, etc.). However, there are always exceptions that require "surgery." I recently needed a workman leaning on a crate. I took one that was standing up with his arms folded, and cut him in half at the waist with a hobby knife. I then filed his torso and legs at an angle so the two pieces met at his back and there was a $^1/_{32}$" gap at his stomach. When I glued the figure back together, he appeared to be leaning forward (see fig. 6-12).

To change the clothing on your figures, either because you do not like the manufacturer's choice of colors or to match a specific time period that you are modeling, you'll have to repaint all or part of the figure. If you want to remove a piece of clothing like a hat, you can file or carve it off but will have to repaint your modification. For example, during the late 1940s most workmen wore caps. Hard hats were found only in building construction or demolition sites. Women's skirts fell below the knee, with the exception of ladies of "ill repute" (as my mother put it). Sneakers were worn by kids and some teenagers, but rarely by adults, unless they were playing tennis. To put period clothes on figures, you can purchase unpainted Preiser figures

and modify or paint their clothing.

Use an assembly-line technique to paint your figures. Leave the figures on the casting sprue, and paint one color at a time over many people, rather than painting all of one figure at a time. Use Polly Scale acrylic paints because of the wide range of colors and flat finish. Before starting to paint, make any modifications to clothing or posture. For example, remove the hard hats cast on most Preiser workers by filing them off altogether or making them look like baseball caps. To modify clothing, remove a figure from the sprue, make the changes with a knife or file, and re-glue it back on the sprue to be painted. You can find the details of my painting process in an article titled "Populate Your Pike," which appeared in the March 1998 issue of *Model Railroader* (order copies by writing to *Model Railroader* magazine, 21027 Crossroads Circle, Waukesha, WI 53187). Figures 6-11 and 6-13 show some of my 1948 painted people.

After modifying and repainting the figures, it is time to install them on the streets of your city. The posture and clothing of each figure should give you an idea where to place it. The next step is to glue it where it belongs. Some manufacturers cast round stands under their figures. Others (like Preiser) provide a sheet of clear

Fig. 6-13. Despite the surrounding concrete, a city's backyards hold surprises. A small garden flourishes (even though Grandma has something to say about harvesting it too soon), and handwashed linens are hung out to dry on a clothesline. Small vignettes like this help liven up the cityscape.

Fig. 6-14. Installing a person on a sidewalk is not that hard. A pair of tweezers position the figure, whose feet have been coated with cyanoacrylate cement. Pressing down with a fingertip will hold it while the glue sets.

plastic from which you can cut stands for each figure. If you use the stand, be sure to paint it the same color as the surface it will rest on to make it less conspicuous. Then glue the figure and stand in place with cyanoacrylate.

I do not use stands, which is one of the reasons I buy Preiser figures that have only feet. To use this type of figure, gently file the soles of its shoes until the paint is removed and the sole is flat. If the figure is to stand on a slope like a sidewalk on a hill, slightly angle the bottom of the feet so it stands vertically. Holding the figure's head with a pair of tweezers, apply a very thin coat of cyanoacrylate (CA) to the bottom of the feet with a bent pin. After putting the figure in place, gently push down on its head with a finger while keeping the tweezers in place (see fig. 6-14). The cyanoacrylate (CA) should set in 10 to 15 seconds. If you exhale several times onto the figure's feet, the

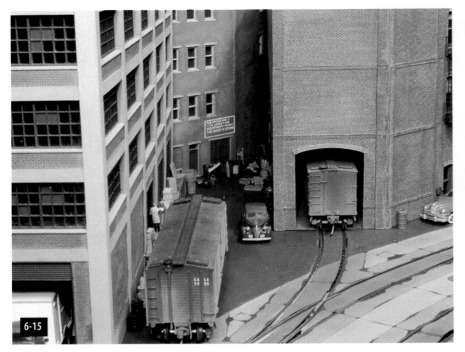

6-15

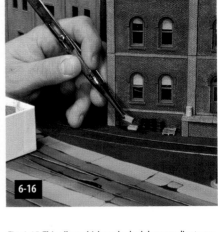

6-16

Fig. 6-15. This alley, which we looked down earlier to see the flats at its back, is now complete. Garbage cans and a parked van line the left side, while a loading dock on the right is filled with crates of produce that workers are moving into the building. The trash and junk are way down at the end of the alley, well off the street.

Fig. 6-16. Here I am placing some crates near a loading dock with a pair of tweezers. My trash box with compartments for crates, garbage cans, oil drums, sacks, and miscellaneous junk travels around the city with me as I dole out its contents.

moisture in your breath will accelerate the setting time. Note, do not use cyanoacrylate accelerator from a spray bottle—the spray could mar the finish on the figure and pavement. Next, remove your finger from the figure while keeping a downward force with the tweezers, and finally remove the tweezers as well. The figure should stand nice and straight. If it falls over, blot the cyanoacrylate off the street and feet and start over. It may take a little practice to get the technique down pat.

Trash and Junk

In all cities there is trash and junk—empty cartons and crates, discarded tires, oil drums, scrap wood—anything that the city's garbage collectors will not pick up on their normal rounds. Where I grew up on Manhattan Island in the 1940s and '50s most trash and junk was kept out of sight in backyards, alleys, and vacant lots. While the same is true today in many urban areas, over the last 30 years entire blocks of some cities have been abandoned. The resulting rows of vacant lots and empty buildings have

become dumping grounds for all kinds of refuse. Most modelers do not have the space for large, abandoned districts, so I recommend confining your trash and junk to backyards and alleys (see fig. 6-15).

Several sources of trash and junk are available to urban modelers:

• Most of us have a scrap box where old parts, kit leftovers, and modeling odds and ends get tossed. If you rummage through yours, you may find parts from old model cars, unidentifiable kit components, bits of scrap wood, plastic, and metal, and who knows what else. Paint old plastic or metal parts Tarnished Black and add a few bits of color to show they were once painted. Dipping metal parts in a chemical blackening chemical will get similar results. Then paint the parts with Rustall, and you can generate some good looking junk in a few minutes.

• Kitchen "junk drawers" (my wife's equivalent of my scrap box) are another source. I can find pieces of aluminum foil, colored scraps of paper, bent staples, "pre-rusted" floral wire, pins—the list is long. Take some foil and crumple it into little bits and

bundles. Bend the staples a little more to look like old pieces of plumbing pipe. Wrap the floral wire around a pencil into little coils. Cut the pins into sections of used pipe. Weather these scraps by darkening some of the parts leaving others bright (the foil), and applying Rustall.

• Buy your trash and junk ready made. Scale Structures Ltd., CMA, Preiser and Selley, to mention a few, make garbage cans, oil drums, pallets, crates, milk cans, etc., which can clutter backyards and alleys. If you cut Plastruct, Evergreen, or Northeastern structural shapes into short pieces, you can make a pile of construction junk or of scrap metal. HO junk piles—coolers, cans, piles of concrete block, broken pallets, etc.—are available as castings from Builders in Scale and Chooch. Paint each item in the pile its original color. Then apply Black Mortar Wash no. 2 (from Chapter 5) to all nonmetal

6-17

6-18

Fig. 6-17. In backyards that are used for gardens or lounging, trash and junk are usually kept out of the usable area. In this yard, tires, oil cans, and miscellaneous junk have been neatly piled next to the fence.

Fig. 6-18. This alley ends in a series of flats pasted to the basement wall. Gluing some trash and junk next to the paper flat helps give it a three-dimensional appearance.

items, and Rustall to the metal pieces.

As your collection of trash and junk grows, make storage boxes for it out of old kit boxes. Divide each box into four or five compartments with scrap cardboard, labeling each for the type of junk it contains—Garbage Cans, Oil Drums, Barrels, Crates, Auto Parts, and whatever you can't identify but looks good. These boxes can travel around the city with you as you add junk to alleys and backyards (see fig. 6-16). By looking at the contents of each compartment, you can tell when your supply of each kind of trash is getting low and make more.

Adding trash and junk to an alley or backyard takes more work than just dumping it. Finish all vegetation in yards, glue down any figures, and place any vehicles in alleys before adding the refuse. Next position different items from your storage box in the alley, but do not glue them down. This allows you to move the trash around until it looks right from where a visitor will be standing. While there are no rules

for placing trash and junk, here are a few guidelines:

• Backyards: If the yard is used by the residents of the building as a place to play ball or relax, trash and junk are usually placed in corners, along the building wall, or next to a fence (if there is one). This allows the trash to be removed by garbage men or scrap dealers, and keeps it out of the middle of the yard, which the residents are using (see fig. 6-17). If the yard is not used, the trash is thrown anywhere that is convenient.

• Alleys: Trash and junk are usually piled along the sides or backs of alleys so that there is a clear path to the surrounding buildings' back doors. This allows door access by people and vehicles as well as a fire exit. Trash cans and dumpsters are usually placed along the alley's wall near its exit so that garbage trucks can get to them easily for pickup. If your alley ends in a flat or backdrop, you can get a three-dimensional effect by placing trash and junk against the flat (see fig. 6-18).

• Vacant lots: These lots are usually

in transition between old buildings that have been demolished and new ones that will be built. Most junk consists of pieces of brick, plumbing, and other small remnants of the demolished structure that the wrecking crew did not clean up. There may even be "transient" items—wrecked cars, car parts, tires and garbage, which are left anonymously at night.

Once you have the trash and junk positioned correctly, draw a map of the alley or yard showing the location of each item. Then remove everything so you can reach all parts of the alley or yard. Starting at the back of the alley, glue each piece of junk in place using cyanoacrylate (CA). Work forward until all of the trash is in place. Then look into the alley or yard from where a visitor would stand and make any necessary corrections.

The details discussed in this chapter—vehicles, people, trash, and junk—are very important in your urban scene. While building, painting, and installing them may seem tedious, the results are well worth the effort.

In every city there is constant change—streets being dug up, old buildings coming down, and new ones under construction. Urban renewal offers very interesting modeling opportunities, such as the demolition scene in this photo. It also gives you the chance to change the look of your city as new kits come on the market.

Updating
Your City

No city is ever static. There is always change going on somewhere. The change may be minor, such as digging up a street. The change can be moderate, such as tearing down an old building that has been condemned. Or the change can be major, such as building a modern high-rise office building. When you are building your city, each of these kinds of change offers a different modeling opportunity:

- Modeling a street repair crew allows you to create an island of detail in your city that is quite different from the surrounding street scenes.
- Adding a building being demolished provides a scene that stands out from the buildings around it.
- Replacing an old structure on your layout with a modern one (or vice versa) allows you to take advantage of new kits on the market with better detail that change the look of your city.

Let's see how to add each kind of change to your cityscape.

Fig. 7-1. Road repairs are the most common form of urban change. This photo is of a typical side street as it looks before the jackhammers go to work. In the following series of photos, we'll look at modeling a road repair gang, step by step.

Fig. 7-2. Remove the buildings on each side of the street to give yourself room to work. The first step is to cut a trench in the street and sidewalk with a hobby knife.

Fig. 7-3. Once the trench is open, pour earth-colored scenic foam into it to look like real dirt underneath. Also remove the manhole cover (just above the trench), drill a real manhole through the pavement, and line its inside with brick paper.

Digging Up a Street

Anyone who has ever lived in a big city, or even a small one, has at some time been exposed to the rattle of jackhammers and the frustration of traffic detours. (When I grew up in New York, they always seemed to dig up streets during the summer, which added noise and dust to the heat and humidity.) Putting a road repair gang in your city is one of the easiest kinds of change to model. Here's how to do it.

Figure 7-1 shows a side street on the urban railroad module discussed in Chapter 4. Note the manhole, which provides access to water pipes, a sewer, electric conduits, and telephone lines—all buried underground. If you think about all of these utilities plus the rain water, road salt from the winter, and dirt that seeps around the edges of the manhole cover, you just know that something will break sooner or later.

In a real city, the only way to repair underground utilities is to dig down to them and fix what has broken—and modelers have to do the same thing. Let's suppose that a new water pipe is needed leading to the building on the right-hand side of the street in fig. 7-1. To install the new

pipe requires digging a trench from the structure's basement to the utility tunnel under the manhole. The first step in creating this scene is to lift the buildings on each side of the street off their alignment pegs and put them in a safe place. You will remember from Chapter 4 that the street surface on the urban railroad is supported above the Homasote by stripwood and foamcore, so that the pavement matches the top of the rails of the in-street trackwork. Using a very sharp hobby knife, cut two parallel lines in the sidewalk and street starting at the wall line of the building to a point two-thirds of the way to the utility tunnel under the manhole (see fig. 7-2). Remove the sidewalk, street surface, and any supporting foamcore between the two cuts until you expose the Homasote under the street.

The next step is to line the opening between the posterboard street surface and Homasote with fast-drying spackling compound to create the walls of the trench. (If your city has streets glued directly onto a base like Homasote, you would make your trench by cutting it out of the base, and could eliminate applying spackling compound.) Then put

some Woodland Scenics fine earth foam along the bottom of the trench so that it looks like the dirt beneath the pavement (see fig. 7-3). Carefully remove any excess foam, accidentally deposited on the surrounding street, with a soft brush. To secure the foam in place, first cut a rectangular hole in a piece of cardboard the same shape as the trench. Holding the cardboard over the trench, very gently spray it with "wet water" (water with a few drops of detergent added as a wetting agent) using the cardboard as a stencil (see fig. 7-4). While the foam is still wet, remove the cardboard and apply Woodland Scenics Scenic Cement to the trench with an eye-dropper (see fig. 7-5). It should flow easily through the foam, gluing it in place.

Then mark the location of the manhole and pry the cover off the street. Drill a hole slightly smaller than the diameter of the manhole cover, which goes through the street and into the Homasote below to a total depth of 1/2". Place the manhole cover on the street a short distance from the hole, with one edge resting on a piece of 4" x 4" scale stripwood. Make a wall for the open manhole from a short piece of brick paper cut

Fig. 7-4. Spray the earth foam-lined trench with "wet water" before adding scenic cement to hold it in place.

Fig. 7-5. Using an eye-dropper, apply scenic cement (matte medium) to the foam.

Fig. 7-6. Add to the "dig" an air compressor, two wheelbarrows, tools, a jackhammer, some earth foam on the street, and four sawhorse barriers to keep away traffic.

to the same height as the depth of the hole you have just drilled, with a length equivalent to the circumference of the manhole. Glue the brick wall in place, thus hiding the space between the posterboard street and the Homasote beneath. Trim the top of the brick paper so that it is flush with the surface of the street.

Next, add construction equipment and details. The first item is a compressor from Selley; paint it Polly Scale Coach Green. Follow this by two wheelbarrows to cart dirt from the open trench to a point in the street where you can position a truck to haul the dirt away. After painting

a little Scenic Cement onto the surface of the street, scatter some earth foam onto it as a trail of dirt accidentally dumped out of the wheelbarrows. Cut the pieces of posterboard and styrene removed from the street and sidewalk into little pieces with jagged edges. Glue them to the dirt along the side of the trench to simulate pieces of concrete and asphalt cut up by the jackhammers. Finally, cement four sawhorses to the street with cyanoacrylate (CA), two at each end of the roadwork to bar traffic from the area. Figure 7-6 shows the open manhole and these details in position.

The final step is to add the road repair gang who are doing the work. You could use a set of Preiser unpainted workers, which includes men working with picks, shovels, and jackhammers. Paint them in colors appropriate to work clothes. (I made one man bare to the waist, since I model late summer.) Make air lines for the jackhammers from soft iron florist's wire, which bends very easily with little spring. One line runs from a worker using a jackhammer back to the compressor, the other from a spare jackhammer lying on the pavement also to the compressor. Paint the air lines Polly Scale AT&SF Red. Then glue three of the workmen in place around the trench—one with a jackhammer, one with a pickax, and one with a shovel. Add a pickup truck sitting on the street near the trench with its tailgate lowered to cart away dirt from the excavation. Add an additional workman shoveling dirt into the back of the truck. Then take a figure with an arm bent in a horizontal position, cut his legs short, and place him in the manhole with his arm resting on the pavement. Finally, place a

Fig. 7-7. Further additions include a truck to haul away the dirt, workers on the road gang, spectators, and a cop keeping traffic from turning into the street. Put the buildings back in place to complete the scene.

Fig. 7-8. Remnants of a building that has been torn down are often visible on the wall of the structure next to it. Add a vacant lot where the building stood, and you add to the sense of change in a city. John Nehrich modeled this scene and wrote an article about it in the November 1998 issue of *Model Railroader*.

Photo by Lou Sassi, courtesy of *Model Railroader* magazine

policeman on the corner directing traffic away from the street. Then put the buildings back on either side of the street to complete the scene, which is shown in fig. 7-7.

Demolishing a Building

Periodically you see TV reports of large buildings being demolished by specially placed explosives. There is a big puff of smoke at the base of the structure, and the whole building collapses in on itself leaving a block of rubble to be cleaned up by bulldozers. This type of demolition is the exception. If you walk through a city, you will see structures being torn down much more frequently by a wrecking ball and men with crowbars and pickaxes.

Luckily, for HO modelers at least, there are two plastic kits on the market of three-story buildings being demolished by this old-fashioned method. Even though they're of European origin, these structures will look at home in older areas of a U.S. city. The first kit, made by Life Like, is a structure with the roof and windows gone. In one wing most of the walls have been torn down, and there is a large pile of rubble where they had been standing. The second kit (from Pola) also depicts a three-story structure, but it is in a more advanced state of demolition. Some of the outer walls are still standing, along with parts of each floor and several

interior partitions. The kit includes a wealth of interior details—radiators, pipes, sinks, toilets, etc.—that are visible. In addition, there is torn wallpaper on interior walls, and the structure has been painted.

The photo at the beginning of this chapter shows a completed Pola kit on Bob Leavitt's layout. Bob placed the structure at the edge of his cityscape right at the front of his railroad so its details could be seen. He took the shine off some of the factory-painted interior walls by spraying them with Dullcote, and weathered the outer walls with chalks. He then fenced off the demolition site, surrounding it with Central Valley plastic board fence to which he added decal and dry-transfer posters and graffiti. He also added Woodland Scenics foam texturing to the mound of dirt and debris at the open

end of the structure, and cut up some scrap styrene to look like pieces of wallboard. Bob placed a large dump truck on the street next to the building to haul away the rubble. If you look at the photo at the beginning of the chapter immediately to the left of the demolished structure, you can see a small, brown DPM building. Bob boarded up its windows with stripwood to make it look deserted. This building is obviously the next target for the wrecker's ball.

A different way to show demolition is to have a vacant lot that once contained a building. All that is left is a wall abutting the next building on the block, which is still standing (see fig. 7-8). An excellent article on modeling this scene, "Ruins That Improve a Model City" by John Nehrich, appeared in the November 1998 issue of *Model Railroader* (you

TYPICAL STEEL BEAM CONFIGURATIONS

Buildings Under Construction

(Sizes are for HO scale)

Type of Steelwork Construction	Shape	Size	Color During	
			Pre-1955	Post-1955
Vertical Column	H	1/4"	Orange	Boxcar Red
Horizontal Beam	I	1/4"	Orange	Boxcar Red
Roof Support*	Lattice	1/4"–3/8"	Orange	Boxcar Red
Diagonal Brace*	Rectangle	1/8"	N/A	Boxcar Red

*Did not come into use until the 1970s

7-9

7-10

Fig. 7-9. Modeling a building under construction is a major task, but the results and what they add to a city are well worth the time. Chuck Bard created this excellent O scale model of a factory going up on the Aberfoyle Junction Railway. It was covered in the August 1998 issue of *Model Railroader*.

Fig. 7-10. The right end of the New Haven cityscape (Chapter 2) originally looked like this. The low gray building and brown tower are part of the same Heljan Brewery as the other structures. Despite color and signs, everything still looked the same.

can get copies of this article by writing to *Model Railroader* magazine, 21027 Crossroads Circle, Waukesha, WI 53187-1612).

Constructing a New Building

Most of the buildings being demolished will be replaced by newer ones. I can remember at the age of eight watching a 30-story office building going up in New York and marveling at the way cranes lifted the steel beams into position, and how the steelworkers walked along the beams to rivet them together. If you want to have a construction scene in your city, there is only one HO kit on the market (from Kibri) that depicts a modern cast-concrete structure being built. So, you will have to scratch-build a "classic" steel structure. While the work is time-consuming, the results are worth the effort. Luckily, there are many styrene and wood structural shapes and styrene and wood sheets of different thickness on the market from which you can fabricate the parts. A steel building skeleton is fairly simple. It consists of

vertical H columns with horizontal I beams at each floor, rising from a poured concrete foundation. Truss beams are also available. They are used to support the roof. The table on the oppposite page gives some guidelines on sizing and painting steelwork. Usually by the time steelwork is being erected, the basement and foundation have been covered. You can make the foundation from .030″ styrene sheet. It consists of a shallow box with four walls and a top. To install it, paint the outside of the box concrete, turn it upside down, and backfill it with Sculptamold painted a color to match the earth of your layout. Then build the steelwork on this foundation. Figure 7-9 shows an O scale factory under construction on the Aberfoyle Junction Railway, which was featured in the August 1998 issue of *Model Railroader* magazine. Chuck Bard scratchbuilt this highly detailed structure as well as the construction cranes.

Kibri makes a wide variety of construction equipment in HO, including earth movers and several types of

cranes capable of lifting steelwork in place. Sheepscot makes detail parts, including tall, etched-brass booms for cranes. Dump trucks large and small are available from Alloy Forms. Most earth movers are painted yellow, while cranes can be yellow, dark red, and light or dark green. Dump trucks can be any color, but black, brown, yellow, and dark red seem to be prevalent.

Swapping Buildings

Probably the most common kind of update to your city will be the complete replacement of one or more buildings. There are a number of reasons that most of us want to swap structures:

• A new well-detailed building kit comes on the market and your city has no space to grow.

• Your existing building is an early modeling effort, and you can do a better job today.

• You are tired of looking at one or more particular buildings, and it is time for a change.

• Any combination of the above

7-11

7-12

Fig. 7-11. I changed the look of New Haven by replacing the two structures on the right with two new buildings made from a Walthers kit and DPM Building Modules, on the left. The photo shows the new structures, which were the same length as the old ones and also spanned the hidden main line that ran under the cityscape.

Fig. 7-12. Here's New Haven as it appears today. The new buildings add variety to the architecture and change the look of the city for the better.

The three questions most commonly asked when a person is planning a swap are "how will it look?" "will it match what I already have?" and "will it fit?"

The answer to the first question is straightforward. Unless the new building has an architecture from a later time than the period that you are modeling, it will probably look fine. Cities are not homogenous, they are a hodgepodge of architecture ranging from the late 1800s to the present day. So swapping a brick building from 1898 with a concrete one from 1950 is no problem, as long as you are modeling 1950 or later.

The answer to the second question is more complex. If the new structure is larger, some surgical alteration is in order. If it is smaller, then put it in location with a parking lot or a plaza to cover the excess space. As an example, let's go back to my New Haven cityscape discussed in the last part of Chapter 2. When I first built the city in 1976, the only large HO urban structure on the market was the Heljan Brewery. I bought a brewery kit and after a lot of cutting and kit-

bashing, turned it into five buildings in the cityscape, three of which are still there. The problem was that even though I painted each building a different color, they all had the same architecture, and the city looked a little artificial. Figure 7-10 shows the right end of the New Haven cityscape as it was originally built. The long two-story structure to the right of the tall beige building, and the narrow four-story tower to its right were the two structures made from Heljan Brewery parts that I wanted to swap out. When I rebuilt the cityscape as part of this book, I had my chance to make the change.

Because each structure in the New Haven cityscape had to abut its neighbors to hide the mainline tracks running through the buildings, the new structures' length had to be exactly equal to the old ones. By a little trial and error, I found that if I removed the front door (and windows above it) at the center of Walthers Roberts Printing Co., I could have a concrete skeleton structure that looked very different from the old piece of Brewery and fit visu-

ally into my late 1940s period very well. I filled the remaining space with a four-story brick structure made from DPM Modules. Figure 7-11 shows the old Heljan structures next to the two new ones.

In order to make installation as easy as possible, I constructed the two new structures as a single unit, with the lower portion of their ends removed so there would be a clear passage for the hidden mainline tracks (see figs. 2-21, 2-22, and 2-23 in Chapter 2). Before installing the new structures, I removed the flat from the back leg of the Heljan structures and glued it onto the back leg of the new structures. I found that I had completely changed the look of New Haven (see fig. 7-12).

There are, of course, other ways besides structures to update your city. New vehicles, people, flats, backdrops, and backyards can all combine to make your city look different. So when you get tired of what you have already built, or when new kits that can enhance the urban scene appear on the market, you can rebuild your city, just like the prototype.

LIST OF MANUFACTURERS MAKING URBAN SCENERY
(Revised for second printing)

The author has compiled the following list of manufacturers that make products suitable to urban modeling *solely to help the readers of this book get started building cities for their model railroads.* While I have attempted to make this list as complete as possible, there are always new manufacturers and products entering the market, as well as existing products to which I have had no exposure. Further, I take *no responsibility* for the *availability* or *quality* of the products listed in this Appendix; nor do I necessarily endorse them.

Name	Ordering Information	Scale	Products
Alexander Scale Models	See your hobby dealer or Walthers catalog(s)	HO, N	D
A-Line	See your hobby dealer or Walthers catalog(s)	HO	D, V
Alloy Forms	See your hobby dealer or Walthers catalog(s)	HO, N	D, V
Alpine Division Models	See your hobby dealer or Walthers catalog(s)	HO	B
American Precision Models	See your hobby dealer or Walthers catalog(s)	HO	V
Ameri-Towne	P. O. Box 239, Nazareth, NJ 18064-0239	O	B, D, M
Aristo Craft Trains	See your hobby dealer or Walthers catalog(s)	G	F, V
Arnold	See your hobby dealer or Walthers catalog(s)	N	BR
Arrowhead Scale Models	See your hobby dealer or Walthers catalog(s)	N	B
Art Griffin	2734 Floral Trail, Michigan City, IN 46360	HO	S
Athearn, Inc.	See your hobby dealer or Walthers catalog(s)	HO	V
Atlas Model Railroad Co., Inc.	See your hobby dealer or Walthers catalog(s)	HO, N	V
Bachmann	See your hobby dealer or Walthers catalog(s)	G, O, HO, N	B, F, V, D
Bar Mills	See your hobby dealer or Walthers catalog(s)	O, S, HO, N	S
Berkshire Valley, Inc.	See your hobby dealer or Walthers catalog(s)	O	B, D, V
Blair Line	See your hobby dealer or Walthers catalog(s)	O, S, HO, N	S
Boley	See your hobby dealer or Walthers catalog(s)	HO	V
Brawa	See your hobby dealer or Walthers catalog(s)	HO, N, Z	D, P, V
Builders In Scale	See your hobby dealer or Walthers catalog(s)	O, S, HO	D, W, F
Busch	See your hobby dealer or Walthers catalog(s)	HO, N, Z	P, V
Cal-Freight	See your hobby dealer or Walthers catalog(s)	N	D
Campbell Scale Models	See your hobby dealer or Walthers catalog(s)	HO, N	B, BR, D, P
Central Valley	See your hobby dealer or Walthers catalog(s)	HO	BR, D
Chooch Enterprises	See your hobby dealer or Walthers catalog(s)	HO, N	D, P
City Classics	See your hobby dealer or Walthers catalog(s)	HO, N	B, M
Classic Metal Cars	See your hobby dealer or Walthers catalog(s)	HO, N	V
Clover House	P. O. Box 62, Sebastopol, CA 95473	HO, N	D, S
Con-Cor	See your hobby dealer or Walthers catalog(s)	HO, N	B, V
Corgi	Model Expo, P. O. Box 229140, 3850 N 29th Terrace, Hollywood, FL 33022	O	V
Country Trains	See your hobby dealer or Walthers catalog(s)	HO, N	R
Creative Model Assoc. (CMA)	See your hobby dealer or Walthers catalog(s)	HO	D
CS Designs	See your hobby dealer or Walthers catalog(s)	All	O
Design Preservation Models	See your hobby dealer or Walthers catalog(s)	O, HO, N	B, M
Detail Associates	See your hobby dealer or Walthers catalog(s)	HO, N	BK, D
Dyna Model Products	See your hobby dealer or Walthers catalog(s)	HO	B, V
Eko	See your hobby dealer or Walthers catalog(s)	HO	F, V
ERTL Co, Inc.	See your hobby dealer or Walthers catalog(s)	O, S, HO	B, V
Evergreen Hill Designs	See your hobby dealer or Walthers catalog(s)	HO	D
Evergreen Scale Models	See your hobby dealer or Walthers catalog(s)	All	O
Faller	See your hobby dealer or Walthers catalog(s)	O, HO, N, Z	B, P, V
Funaro & Camerlengo	See your hobby dealer or Walthers catalog(s)	HO	B
GHQ	See your hobby dealer or Walthers catalog(s)	N	V
Grandt Line	See your hobby dealer or Walthers catalog(s)	G, O, S, HO, N	D, F
Greg's Garage	6266 Thistle Drive, Saginaw, MI 48603	HO	V
Heljan	See your hobby dealer or Walthers catalog(s)	HO, N	B
Herpa	See your hobby dealer or Walthers catalog(s)	HO	D, V
Holgate & Reynolds	See your hobby dealer or Walthers catalog(s)	All	P
IMEX	See your hobby dealer or Walthers catalog(s)	HO	V
International Hobby Corp.	See your hobby dealer or Walthers catalog(s)	O, HO, N	B, D, F, S, V
JL Innovative Designs	See your hobby dealer or Walthers catalog(s)	HO, N	S
Jordan Products	See your hobby dealer or Walthers catalog(s)	HO	V
Kibri	See your hobby dealer or Walthers catalog(s)	HO, N, Z	B, F, P, V
K-Line	See your hobby dealer or Walthers catalog(s)	G, O	B, V
Korber Models	See your hobby dealer or Walthers catalog(s)	HO	B
Life Like	See your hobby dealer or Walthers catalog(s)	G, O, HO, N	B, D, F
Lionel	See your hobby dealer or Walthers catalog(s)	O	B, V

Name	Ordering Information	Scale	Products
Lonestar Models	See your hobby dealer or Walthers catalog(s)	HO	V
Magnuson Models	See your hobby dealer or Walthers catalog(s)	HO, N	V
Main Street Graphics	See your hobby dealer or Walthers catalog(s)	HO, N	W
Märklin	See your hobby dealer or Walthers catalog(s)	Z	B, V
Master Creations	See your hobby dealer or Walthers catalog(s)	O, HO	B, D
Metal Miniatures	See your hobby dealer or Walthers catalog(s)	HO, N	D, V
Micro Engineering	See your hobby dealer or Walthers catalog(s)	HO, N	B, BR, D
Micro Trains	See your hobby dealer or Walthers catalog(s)	N	V
Microscale Industries	See your hobby dealer or Walthers catalog(s)	O, HO, N	S
MilePost Model Works	See your hobby dealer or Walthers catalog(s)	G, O	D
Mini Highways	See your hobby dealer or Walthers catalog(s)	G, O	P
Model Memories	P. O. Box 692, Bethel, CT 06801	HO, N	D
Model Power	See your hobby dealer or Walthers catalog(s)	G, O, HO, N	B, F, S, V
Model Railways	See your hobby dealer or Walthers catalog(s)	HO	D
Mountains in Minutes	See your hobby dealer or Walthers catalog(s)	G, HO	S
NJ International	See your hobby dealer or Walthers catalog(s)	HO, N	D, F, V
Noch	See your hobby dealer or Walthers catalog(s)	O, HO, N, Z	D, F, P, V
Northeastern Scale Models	See your hobby dealer or Walthers catalog(s)	O, HO, N	B, O
On-Trak	See your hobby dealer or Walthers catalog(s)	O, HO	D, V
Period Miniatures	See your hobby dealer or Walthers catalog(s)	N	B, D
Pikestuff	See your hobby dealer or Walthers catalog(s)	HO	B, D
Piko	See your hobby dealer or Walthers catalog(s)	G, HO, N	B, P
Pioneer Valley Models	P. O. Box 4928, Holyoke, MA 01041	O	B, D
Pirate Models, Ltd.	See your hobby dealer or Walthers catalog(s)	HO, N	V
Plastruct, Inc.	See your hobby dealer or Walthers catalog(s)	All, O, HO, N, Z	B, D, O, P, V
Pola	See your hobby dealer or Walthers catalog(s)	G, HO, N	B, D, F, V
Praline	See your hobby dealer or Walthers catalog(s)	HO	V
Preiser	See your hobby dealer or Walthers catalog(s)	G,O,S,HO,N,Z	D, F, P, V
Q-Car Company	See your hobby dealer or Walthers catalog(s)	O	D
Quality Products Co.	See your hobby dealer or Walthers catalog(s)	HO, N	S
Rail Power Products	See your hobby dealer or Walthers catalog(s)	HO	V
Resin Unlimited	See your hobby dealer or Walthers catalog(s)	HO	V
Rix Products	See your hobby dealer or Walthers catalog(s)	HO, N	B, BR, D
Roco	See your hobby dealer or Walthers catalog(s)	HO, N	V
S L M	P. O. Box 28047 Baltimore, MD 21239	HO	B
S&S Hobby Products	See your hobby dealer or Walthers catalog(s)	HO, N	P
Scale Scenics	See your hobby dealer or Walthers catalog(s)	HO, N	R, V, D
Scale Structures Ltd.	See your hobby dealer or Walthers catalog(s)	HO	B, D, V
Scale Works Models	See your hobby dealer or Walthers catalog(s)	All	P
Selley Finishing Touches	See your hobby dealer or Walthers catalog(s)	HO	D, F, S
Sheepscott Products	See your hobby dealer or Walthers catalog(s)	HO	B, D, V
Simpson	See your hobby dealer or Walthers catalog(s)	G	D
Smalltown USA	See your hobby dealer or Walthers catalog(s)	HO	B, P, D
Sylvan Scale Models	32229 Sylvan Rd., RR #2, Parkhill, ON, N0M-2K0 Canada	HO, N	B
Triangle Scale Models	See your hobby dealer or Walthers catalog(s)	S	D
Trident	See your hobby dealer or Walthers catalog(s)	HO	V
Trucks-N-Stuff	See your hobby dealer or Walthers catalog(s)	HO	V
Twin Whistle Sign & Kit Co.	60 Silk St., Arlington, MA 02174	O, S, HO	B, D, S
Vintage Reproductions	See your hobby dealer or Walthers catalog(s)	HO, N	D
Vista Scenics	See your hobby dealer or Walthers catalog(s)	O, HO	D
Vollmer	See your hobby dealer or Walthers catalog(s)	HO, N, Z	B, P
Wheel Works	See your hobby dealer or Walthers catalog(s)	HO	V
Whiteground Model Works	See your hobby dealer or Walthers catalog(s)	O, HO, N	B, S
Wiking	See your hobby dealer or Walthers catalog(s)	HO, N	V
Williams Bros., Inc.	See your hobby dealer or Walthers catalog(s)	HO	V
Wm. K. Walthers	P. O. Box 3039, Milwaukee, WI 53201-3039	O, HO, N	B, BK, P, V, S, W
Woodland Scenics	See your hobby dealer or Walthers catalog(s)	All, HO, N	B, D, O, P, S, V

+---+
| Product Key |
| |
| B   Building kits   O   Structural shapes and scenic supplies |
| BK   Backdrops   P   Wall/Stone paper, pavement, and sidewalks |
| BR   Bridges   R   Road signs |
| D   Details   S   Signs: Advertising, electric, billboard, wall |
| F   Figures   V   Vehicles |
| M   Building modules   W   Windows and window material |
+---+

Note: It is recommended that readers contact their hobby dealer first for any of the products in this Appendix. However, addresses have been given for those manufacturers who sell by direct mail or are not listed in available industry catalogs.